ABEL JANSZOON TASMAN

His Life and Voyages

JAMES BACKHOUSE WALKER

ABEL JANSZOON TASMAN

Read before the Royal Society of Tasmania on the 25th November
1895

by

James Backhouse Walker, F.R.G.S.

Tasmania:

William grahame, Jun., Government Printer, Hobart.

1896

PREFACE.

No life of the first circumnavigator of Australia has hitherto appeared in English. Nothing has been accessible to the English reader but an abstract of one voyage and a few lines in biographical dictionaries. This is scarcely surprising, when we consider how careless Tasman's own countrymen have been of his fame. Fifty years ago all that had been printed in his own country consisted of short abstracts of a few voyages, and these were hidden away in bulky collections. Even the date and place of his birth were matter for conjecture .and dispute. Things are somewhat better now. Thirty-five years ago the complete journal of his famous voyage of 1642 was published in Holland, and we are now promised a sumptuous *fac simile* edition of the original manuscript, with notes by two eminent scholars, and with an English translation.

Moreover, patient searchers in the Dutch Colonial Archives have for years past been laboriously gleaning scattered particulars respecting him, and the results of their investigations have been printed from time to time in the transactions of Dutch learned societies, and in other places. It has thus become possible to piece together a fairly connected account of the great navigator's life.

But after all available information has been made use of, the result is disappointing. The man himself remains for the most part an indistinct figure. Personal details are few. The facts are mostly dry and meagre, gathered from formal official despatches and dusty registers. The material is wanting for a biography which would give a clear and sharply defined picture of the man as he lived.

It is possible, however, to attain what is of even more interest. We can arrive at a just estimate of his work as a discoverer, and of his place among the great navigators of the

world. The discovery of Tasmania and New Zealand was no chance adventure. It was the result of a steady policy. It was the outcome of the adventurous energy which in the 16th and 17th centuries created the Dutch Republic; gave to Holland her Colonial Empire; and--not content with her possession of the Eastern Archipelago--sent out her sailors to search for a New world in the unknown regions of the mysterious South. Tasman and Visscher are but types of the men who won for their country her once proud position of mistress of the seas.

In the following pages an attempt has been made not merely to give all that is known of Tasman's life and work, but to present that work in proper historical perspective.

I desire to acknowledge generally my obligation to the authors whose names appear in the list appended to this paper, particularly to Messrs. Dozy, Heeres, Van Boekeren, and Leupe. Also to Sir Edward Braddon for his courtesy in having, when Agent-General for Tasmania, obtained for me valuable information from Holland. Especially to Mr. J. E. Heeres, of the Dutch State Archives at The Hague, for his generous kindness in placing at my disposal manuscript notes of his researches in the old Colonial Records--notes containing interesting details which have never before appeared in print. And, lastly, to the Treasurer, Sir Philip Fysh, for authorising the printing of this paper at the Government Press of the Colony. It is fitting that the first English biography of Tasman should be offered to Australian readers by the country which he discovered and which bears his name.

JAMES B. WALKER.

Hobart, January, 1896.

MAPS.

[MAPPE-MONDE, CIRCA 1630

(From the Atlas of Janssonius; Amsterdam, circa 1630.) Shows the Terra Australis Nondum Cognita, as supposed before Tasman's discoveries. The figures in the border of the map represent: (1) The Seven Planets. (2) The Seven Wonders of the World. (3) The Four Elements. (4) The Four Seasons.

[MAP OF TASMAN'S VOYAGES, 1642 AND 1644

(Reduced from the *fac simile* in Mr. Jacob Swart's edition of the Journal of 1642; Amsterdam, 1860.) The original map--which is elaborately coloured--is probably the work of the Pilot-Major Frans Visscher. [See Bibliographical Notes; Manuscript Maps, No. 1.

MAP OF ANTHONY VAN DIEMENSLANDT

(From Messrs. F. Muller and Co.'s reproduction of the map in Tasman's Journal.) The original map--which is carefully coloured--is contained in the Manuscript Journal preserved in the State Archives at The Hague, and described in the Bibliographical Notes as R.A. 2.

INTRODUCTION.

The modern era of maritime discovery may be said to begin with the work of Prince Henry of Portugal, surnamed "The Navigator" (1394-1460). Prince Henry devoted his life to the furtherance of geographical discovery. He was inspired by the hope of finding the sea-route to the East, and winning for his country the rich trade of India and Cathay. During forty years he sent out from Lagos fleet after fleet bound for the exploration of the coasts of Africa. Further and further south into the unknown and dreaded Atlantic his caravels pushed their way, until at his death, in 1460, his captains had reached the mouth of the Gambia beyond Cape Verde, and had colonised the Azores. The discoveries made under this Prince's inspiring influence were the stepping-stone to the great voyages which marked the close of the century. Following the initiative of Henry, the bold genius of Columbus conceived the splendid idea of finding the East by sailing west; and, in 1492, when he fell upon America, he believed that he had reached the further shores of India. Five years later Henry's countryman, Vasco da Gama, in a voyage almost as important as that of Columbus, doubled the Cape of Good Hope, and opened the gates of the sea-way to Calicut and the East. Pope Alexander the Sixth by his famous Bull apportioned the world between the discoverers--allotting the western half to Spain, and the eastern to Portugal. From that time the gold and silver of the West were poured into the lap of Spain while Portugal gathered in as her sole property the rich profits of the coveted trade of the East. For well nigh a century the two nations enjoyed a practical monopoly of the regions which the daring of their sailors had won. Spain, in particular, through the wealth she acquired from her American possessions, became the dominant power in the world, and the mistress of the sea. Her fall from that high eminence was due to her arrogant greed for universal dominion, and her attempt to crush a free nation of traders.

In the 15th and 16th centuries the Netherlands--the Low Countries of common English parlance--were the most prosperous nation in Europe. While other nations exhausted themselves in war, they devoted themselves to the arts of peace. In agriculture they were far in advance of all other countries of the time, The Flemish weavers were the first in the world, and their looms supplied England and all Europe with the best linen and woollen fabrics. In an age when salted provisions were almost the sole winter diet of all classes, the fisheries of the North Sea were nearly as important as the manufactures of Flanders. These fisheries were well nigh monopolised by the Hollanders, and were a rich mine of wealth to the northern towns, while they trained a hardy and daring race of sailors. In addition to their manufactures and their fisheries, the Dutch had become the traders and carriers of the European world. It was Dutch ships and Dutch sailors that distributed throughout Europe the treasures brought by Spanish and Portuguese fleets from the East and West Indies.

The Netherlands were an appanage of the Spanish crown. But, the rich manufacturing and trading cities of Flanders and Holland enjoyed considerable liberties and powers of local self-government, granted to them from time to time by their over-lords in exchange for heavy annual payments. It was the attempt of the Spanish king Philip the Second to abolish the charters of their towns, to stamp out their liberties, and to suppress the Reformed Religion by means of the Inquisition, that led to the rise of the Dutch Republic, and the long and cruel war with the revolted Provinces, which lasted eighty years (1566-1648), and finally resulted in the humiliation of Spain.

The Dutch revolt forms one of the most striking epochs in history. It was the first blow struck in modern times for human freedom and liberty of conscience against the despotism of kings and the intolerance of priests. The power of the strongest empire in the world was put forth to crush the revolted citizens. Treachery, torture, and massacre were freely and ruthlessly employed. The butcheries of the Duke of Alva still stand out pre-eminent in the bloody annals of tyranny and persecution. The story, as we read it in the graphic pages of Motley, bristles with deeds of ferocious cruelty and blood.

The struggle would have been hopeless, but that their extremity taught the Dutch to find their strength upon the sea. Powerless before their enemies on land, the patriots took to the ocean. In small vessels their hardy sailors cut off the Spanish supplies, made daring descents on sea-coast towns; and in process of time set themselves to work to strike Spain in her most vulnerable part, her commerce with the New World, from which she drew her wealth. The Beggars of the Sea, as the Dutch rovers styled themselves, became the terror of the richly laden galleons and haughty fleets of Spain. Not only did they cut off the supplies of gold and silver from the New World on which the Spanish King depended, but in the spoils which they wrested from the enemy and in the trade which they were continually extending they found the means for their country to carry on the conflict. England, almost equally in danger from Spanish designs, made common cause against the enemy. Even when the countries were not at open war, Drake and the English seamen acknowledged no peace with Spain beyond the Line, but captured her ships `and sacked her settlements on the Spanish Main, returning home laden with treasure. Foiled in his disastrous attempt to conquer England with his Great Armada, Philip was equally unsuccessful in his efforts to destroy the Dutch commerce. In vain did he prohibit the Hollanders from trading with his dominions. In vain did he from time to time lay embargoes on their ships, and send thousands of their sailors to languish in the dungeons of the Inquisition. The bold Hollanders only replied by vigorous reprisals. They mocked at his prohibitions, and continued to carry on an ever increasing and enormously profitable illicit trade. Dutch and English privateers triumphantly swept the seas and harried the Spaniards at their pleasure. Subjugated Flanders had become an obedient Spanish province; her rich merchants had fled, and her people were starving in a desolated country. But the unconquered United Provinces of the north were actually profiting by the war, and every day growing richer and more powerful.

The long struggle on the seas, and its successful issue, roused both in England and Holland an insatiable spirit of adventure. In England this spirit found its outlet in privateering or piratical exploits, such as those of Hawkins and Drake; or in romantic expeditions, such as that of Raleigh to Guiana; and led, in its ultimate development, to the establishment of our Colonial and Indian Empire.

In Holland the adventurous spirit received a strong stimulus from the blind and stupid policy of the Spanish king. For a hundred years--ever since the discovery of the Cape route to the East Indies--Lisbon had been the great centre of the eastern trade. It was thither the Dutch traders came to bring wheat, fish, and other products of Northern Europe, and to carry away in return and distribute the spices and merchandise of the East. In 1594 Philip--who had some time before acquired the crown of Portugal--closed the port of Lisbon, and prohibited Dutch and English ships, even under a neutral flag, from trading with any part of his empire. The blow not only failed of its effect, but recoiled on the striker. It ruined Lisbon; crippled Spain; and made the Dutch East Indian Empire. With a sagacious daring the Hollanders immediately formed the steady resolve to find these eastern treasures for themselves, and wrest the trade from their enemies.

Their first attempt to reach the Indies was discouraging. It was a favourite idea in those days that a short and practicable route to China and India could be found by the north-east passage round the north of Europe. To find this passage and take the Portuguese in the rear was the object of the first Dutch enterprise. The expedition proved disastrous getting no further than Nova Zembla. Two subsequent expeditions in the same direction met with no better fate.

Baffled in their efforts to find a passage through the frozen seas of the North, the Dutch turned their attention to the old route round the Cape. The merchants of Amsterdam formed a company, under the quaint name of "The Company of Far Lands," and fitted out four vessels, the largest 400 tons, and the smallest only 30 tons burden. The little fleet-sailed from the Texel 2nd April, 1595. After a fifteen months' voyage it reached Java, and laid the foundation of the Dutch eastern trade. From this time numerous new companies were formed in Holland: every year fresh fleets left for the east, many of them returning with rich cargoes, and making enormous profits. In spite of the violent attacks of the Spaniards and Portuguese, the Dutch steadily pushed their way in the Eastern Archipelago, and made reprisals on their enemies with telling effect. Their humane and prudent conduct contributed greatly to their success in establishing trade relations with the native princes, by whom the Portuguese were detested for their cruelty, arrogance, and overbearing behaviour.

The English had now entered into competition with the Dutch in the India trade, and in 1600 the first English East India Company was founded. But the English company found their rivals too powerful. In 1602 the various companies in Holland agreed to cease their mutual competition and unite. This was the beginning of the famous Dutch East India Company, which, on 20th March, 1602, received from the States-General a charter for twenty-one years, giving it an exclusive monopoly of the trade with the East. The company had a capital of six and a half millions of florins or £550,000, more than eight times that of its English rival. It was managed by a body of seventeen directors, known as the Council of Seventeen.

The Dutch had already (1602) established themselves permanently in Java. Here they founded the city of Batavia, which became the centre of their trade and the residence of the Governor-General of their Eastern possessions. They established factories in Malabar, drove the Spaniards from Amboyna and took possession of the island, wrested Malacca from the Portuguese, and expelled the same nation froth the Moluccas or Spice Islands. In 1621, less than twenty years after its foundation, the Company had a practical monopoly of the trade in cloves, nutmegs, cinnamon, and other products of the Archipelago. The Portuguese had been driven out, and, England only waged an obstinate but unsuccessful rivalry. In 1638 the Dutch supplanted the Portuguese in Japan, and in 1656 got possession of the island of Ceylon.

In a work by Sir Walter Raleigh, entitled "Observations touching Trade and Commerce with the Hollanders and other Nations," presented to King James in the year 1603, we find a striking picture of the commerce of the Netherlands as compared with that of England.

Raleigh attributes the sudden and astonishing rise of the Netherlanders, among other causes, to the "embargoing and confiscating of their ships in Spain, which constrained them, and gave them courage to trade by force into the East and West Indies, and in Africa, where they employ 180 ships and 8700 mariners." (This, it should be noted, was only seven years after the first Dutch vessel had reached Java.) Sir Walter gives a number of interesting particulars respecting the extent of Dutch trade. He says, "We send into the Eastern kingdoms [of Europe] yearly but 100 ships; the Low Countries 3000. They send into France, Portugal, and Italy from the Eastern kingdoms through the Sound and our narrow seas 2000 ships; we, none. They trade with 500 or 600 ships into our country; we, with 40 ships to three of their towns. They have as many ships as eleven kingdoms of Christendom, let England be one. They build yearly 1000 ships, having not one timber tree growing in their own country, nor home-bred commodities to lade 100 ships, yet they have 20,000 ships and vessels, and all employed." In shipbuilding and seamanship also the Dutch sailors in those days were the superiors of the English, for Sir Walter says that while an English ship of a hundred tons required a crew of thirty men, the Hollanders would sail a ship of the same size with ten men.

We are accustomed to dwell on the naval exploits of Drake, Hawkins, and Frobisher, on the enterprise of the Elizabethan sailors and merchant-adventurers, and on the marvellous success of-our own great East India Company. We have good reason to feel pride in the deeds of the gallant English seamen of those days, and in the trade which in later times has carried the English flag into every sea. But we are apt to forget how comparatively recent is the predominant position of England in commerce and in naval power. In the 17th century it was the Dutch who were the sailors and the merchants of the world and the masters of the sea. Not London, but Amsterdam, was the great emporium for the products of East and West, the centre of the world's trade, and the richest city on the globe. The commerce of Europe and of the world was in the hands of the merchants of the Low Countries, who had a hundred ships afloat for every one owned by Englishmen.

TASMAN'S LIFE AND VOYAGES

I.--YOUTH AND EARLY VOYAGES, 1603-1638.

It was in the midst of the Eighty Years. War, in the year after the foundation of the Company in whose service he was to win his fame, and in the same year that Sir Walter Raleigh presented to King James his memorial on the trade of the Hollanders, that Abel Janszoon Tasman stepped onto this world's stage. He was born in the little inland village of Luytjegast, in the province of Groningen, in the year 1603. Groningen is the most north-easterly province of Holland, and formed part of the ancient Friesland. It is flat, even for proverbially flat Holland. The highest hill, the Doeseberg, rises to a height of only 35 feet above the level of the ocean, and some of the country lies even below the sea level. It is protected from the furious inroads of the North Sea by magnificent dykes of timber and stone. Behind these massive ramparts stretch wide and fertile fields and meadows, rich in agricultural and dairy produce. The cultivators, who hold their lands under a species of tenant right, are at present the richest and most prosperous peasant farmers in the whole of Europe. In Roman times the Frisians occupied the country from the Elbe to the Rhine, including the extensive tract now covered by the Zuyder Zee, over which the sea burst so late as the thirteenth century. They were sea rovers as well as cattle herdsmen, and were distinguished for their fierce independence and indomitable love of liberty. They were one of the tribes that took part in the conquest of Britain. At this day the Frisian language, spoken by a handful of people is the most nearly related of all Low German dialects to the English, and the men are nearest to the English in blood. The Frieslanders are of a different race from the inhabitants of Holland proper. The typical Dutchman is squat and short-legged; the Frieslander, tall, yellow-haired, blue-eyed, and of powerful build. We may fairly believe that Tasman belonged to this tall, bold, and impetuous race, who supplied no small proportion of the hardy fishermen and sailors whose daring made Holland a great sea power.

We have no information as to the Tasman family, but it is to be presumed that its social status was a humble one. How Abel came by the surname which is now world-renowned is a matter of dispute. In the Luytjegast district family names were unknown until the beginning of this century. The son added to his own christian name the christian name of his father; thus, Abel, the son of John, became Abel Janszoon, and by this name simply Tasman is often designated in the old records. A nickname was often acquired, derived from some personal peculiarity, from a trade, a sign, or a ship. It has been conjectured that either Abel Jansz or his father took the name Tasman or Taschman from a boat or vessel named the *Tasch* (bag or net), belonging to the family.[*1]

Of young Abel's early life in the flat polders or meadows of Luytjegast there is no record. The boy would see little or nothing of the horrors of the war which for forty years had been desolating a great part of the Low Countries. The most desperate part of the struggle was over with the death of Alexander of Parma. The gloomy bigot and tyrant, Philip the Second, was dead. Flanders had fallen, and had become an obedient and desolate Spanish province, under the rule of the Archduke Albert and his wife Isabella of Spain; but the United Provinces, under Prince Maurice of Nassau, son of William the Silent, were not only holding their own against the Spaniards, but were daily growing in prosperity and power. When young Abel was six years old they had succeeded in wringing from their exhausted enemy a twelve years' truce, with the acknowledgment of the Republic, and of its right to carry on the India trade. The boy's imagination must have been often stirred by tales of the daring deeds of the Beggars of the Sea, and the heroic resistance of Hollanders and Zeelanders to the mighty power of Spain. Not less must his spirit of adventure have been stimulated by the stories that drifted to his quiet village telling of the riches of India, of the Spice Islands, and of far Cathay. Small wonder that the old sea-roving Frisian blood asserted itself, and that Abel Jansz; like the majority of Hollanders in that age, found his vocation as a sailor. That he had managed to acquire some education is evident from the fact that he had at least leaned to write, a somewhat rare accomplishment in those days fore persons in his humble station.

It is not unlikely that in the fisheries of the North Sea, that nursery of daring sailors, he served his first apprenticeship to the ocean. But the adventurous spirit was strong within him, and it was natural that he should soon find his way to

[*1) In the Archives of Hoorn there is a document relating to a ship called the *Tasch*, of which the skipper was Cornelis Gerritszoon Taschman.]

Amsterdam, the centre of the commerce of the world, eager to seek his fortune in the rich eastern lands which his countrymen had won. He had married young--either in his native province or in Amsterdam--and his wife, Claesjie Heyndricks, had died, leaving him an only daughter. When we get the first definite information respecting him he was a widower, living in the Terketelsteeg (Tarkettle Lane), one of the poorest quarters of Amsterdam. Here, on the 27th December, 1631, he married his second wife, Jannetjie Tjaers.[*1] He was not encumbered with property,--at least his name does not appear in the contemporary register of assessment for the half per cent. tax. His wife was not greatly his superior in social position, and could not sign the marriage register. She belonged to a working-class family,--her father being a powder-maker, and her brother a sailor, like her husband. The family were not, however, altogether without means. They were owners of one, if not two, small houses in Amsterdam. The young couple began life in a more respectable locality than Tarkettle Lane, setting up house in the Palm-street. It cannot have been long after his marriage that Abel Jansz, then 28 or 29 years old, made what was probably his first voyage to the East Indies, in the service of the Dutch East India Company. That shortly after this time he was in the service of the Company in the Eastern Seas we know from independent evidence. Mr. Heeres has found in the old Colonial archives two declarations signed by Tasman in 1634, which inform us of his rapid rise, during the space of two years at most, from the position of a simple sailor to that of master of a ship. In May he was mate of the ship *Weesp* (*Wasp*), trading from Batavia in Java, to Amboyna in the Moluccas. In July the Governor of Amboyna appointed him master--" skipper" was the term in those days--of the jachtt[*2] *Mocha*.

Tasman was therefore employed in the spice trade, the chief centre of which was the Moluccas or Spice Islands, and especially Amboyna and the Banda Isles, the native home of the nutmeg and the clove. In these days it is difficult for us to understand the value which our forefathers, even down to the end of the 17th century, set upon eastern apices-- pepper, cinnamon, ginger, nutmeg, and especially cloves. It has been remarked that at banquets in England in the Middle Ages a place next to the spice-box was more coveted than the proverbial place above the salt. This may probably be explained by the fact of the little variety of food possible during the Middle Ages, when (in the winter especially) all classes had to live mostly on salt provisions--especially salt fish--and had hardly any fresh vegetables, until the Dutch taught Europe how to grow them. Before the discovery of the route round the Cape, a pound of spice was often worth as much as a. quarter of wheat. After Da Gama's voyage the trade remained for a century in the hands of the Portuguese, and the monopoly yielded them enormous profit, sometimes as much as fifty-fold. The hope of getting possession of this coveted trade was the chief incentive to Dutch efforts to reach the Indiea. Pepper, ginger, and cinnamon were too widely grown to enable them to command a monopoly, and in these articles the English East India Company was able with more or less success to divide the trade with the Dutch. It was otherwise with the more valued spices, such as nutmeg and cloves. These were limited to a few of the East India Islands. Cloves in particular grew nowhere but on two or three islands of the Moluccas. To secure the monopoly of these the Dutch accordingly bent all their energies. In 1605 they succeeded in driving the Portuguese out of Amboyna, and obtaining the mastery of the whole of the Moluccas. The English East India Company kept up an obstinate rivalry, but the Dutch met them with determined hostility. They attacked the English factories on small pretext, captured their vessels, and, after the massacre of a number of English traders at Amboyna, in 1623, finally excluded their rivals from all share in the trade. This contest for the spice trade was the origin and chief cause of the long and bitter enmity between the two nations. To such lengths did the Dutch go that some years later they ruthlessly rooted up the clove plantations on all the islands of the Moluccas except Amboyna and Banda. Here alone did they allow the clove to be produced, in order that they might enhance the price and make certain of preserving their monopoly.

[*1) The following is a translation of the entry in the Register of the Amsterdam Church, dated 27 December, 1031:--Abel Janss. of Luttiejast, seaman, aged 28 years, living in the Terketelsteech, widower of Claesjie Heyndricks; and Jannetie Tjaers, of Amsterdam, aged 21 years; her sister Geertie Tjaers being present, living in the Palm-street. [In the margin.] Dirckie Jacobs, the mother, consents to the said marriage, as Jan Jacobs attests.]

[*2) "Jacht," a small ship of from 100 to 200 tons burden.]

But to return to Tasman. It is evident that his singular capacity had soon made itself evident to the colonial authorities, for in August, 1635, we find the simple sailor of three years before, now as "Commandeur Abel," cruising at the head of a fleet of small vessels (*kiels*) to protect the jealously guarded monopoly from foreign intrusion, and generally to harass the ships of hostile European rivals in the waters of Amboyna arid the Banda Sea. In September, 1636, he was on his way back to Batavia, the centre of Dutch rule and the residence of the Governor-General of the Indies. On his arrival, he found himself involved in difficulties with his crew. They cited him before the Chief Magistrate's Court complaining that while cruising in the Banda Sea he had, presumably in the interests of his own pocket, stinted them of their necessary allowance of rations. As he was acquitted by the Court, which was sufficiently experienced in such matters, we may conclude that he was unjustly accused: at least we may give him the benefit of the doubt.

He was now bent on revisiting the home country, and to accomplish this he was ready to accept for the time a subordinate post, and accordingly shipped as mate on board the *Banda*. The *Banda* was the flagship of a homeward-bound fleet (*retour vloot*) of several sail. Her skipper was Matthys Quast, a bold and capable sailor, of whom we shall hear more presently. When on the point of sailing, on 30th December, 1636, the officers and crew, 111 in number, were required to make a declaration, which is interesting as illustrative of the troubled state of the times, of the dangers of war, and the prevalence of privateering. It also shows the survival of the ancient usage--a part of the old maritime law of the 13th century, the Roles d'Oleron--which gave to the ship's Council, and even to the common sailors, a voice in the control of the voyage. By this declaration--to which the whole 111 set their signatures or marks--the Governor, skipper, merchant, mates, officers, soldiers, and seamen, presently appointed and sailing on the ship *Banda*, solemnly promised that, in view of the Spanish men-of-war and the privateers of Dunkirk, they would in no wise pass through the English Channel, but would hold their course round England, Ireland, and Scotland, so that they might in safety make the harbours of the Fatherland.

The *Banda* arrived at the Texel on 1st August, 1637, after a seven months' voyage. Tasman remained at Amsterdam for some months with his wife Jannetie, who had recovered from an illness so serious that she had made her will. This will is still in existence. It was drawn up on 18th December, 1636, by the Notary, Pieter Barcman. It recites that the worthy Jannetje Tjercks, wife of Abel Jansz Tasman, citizen, was then lying ill in bed, but was of good memory and understanding. Her residence was at the corner of the Palm cross-street on the Braeck. Should the testatrix die without issue, then, after certain bequests to the poor, she constituted her sister, Geertje Tjercks, her sole legatee. There is no mention of her husband or of the little step-daughter, Claesjen. We need not therefore assume that there had been any quarrel between the married pair. The absence of Abel in the

Indies, from which return was so uncertain, may explain why the wife should leave her property to relations on the spot.

Meantime Abel and his brothers-in-law appeared before the Amsterdam magistrates with the object of selling the family house in the Palm-street for 500 florins. For some reason the contract was cancelled, and the family retained the house until 1650, when Powels Barentsz, in his own name, and as attorney for his brother-in-law Tasman, who was then in the Indies, conveyed the property to Andries Barents.

After a stay of some nine months in Amsterdam, Abel Jansz once more set his face eastwards. He entered into a new ten years' engagement with the Company, and in consideration of this he was allowed to take his wife with him--the Council of Seventeen having just passed a new regulation whereby the chief officers were permitted to take their wives to the East Indies, provided they were lawfully wedded, were of good lives, and could show good credentials. Tasman was put in command of the fly-ship**[*1]** *Engel* (*Angel*), fitted out by the Amsterdam Chamber. VThe *Engel* sailed from the Texel, 15th April, 1638, and arrived at Batavia on 11th October following. The skipper's pay was 60 guilders (£5) per month. On arrival at Batavia he was continued in his post for three years at an increased pay of 80 guilders (£6 13s. 4d.) per month.

II.--VOYAGES IN JAPAN SEAS, &c., 1639-1642.

It is in the year following his return to Batavia, some six years after his first voyage thither, that we find Abel Jansz first chosen to take a prominent part in a discovery expedition.

The enterprise of the early Dutch governors in their efforts to open up new trade for their Company was ceaseless. Jan Pieterszoon Coen, Governor-General between 1618 and 1629, was the most illustrious, and the one who did most to consolidate the Dutch power. He it was who built the fort at Batavia, and fixed the centre of government there. He it was who in Java baffled the English, and overmastered them in the Moluccas. During his rule Dutch ships first made the coast of Australia. After Coen, the most famous governor--he who showed the greatest energy in his persistent search for new lands and new markets--was Antony van Diemen, the Governor-General who was in power when Tasman returned to the Indies, and with whom his-fame will be for ever associated.

[*1) Fly-ships (fluit) were long quick-sailing ships, of light draught, varying from 200 to 400 tons burden. Fly-ships were first built at Hoop in 1594.

Early in the career of the Dutch Company in the Eastern Archipelago the Directors had east longing eyes towards the powerful kingdom of the Great Khan--the Cathay whose wonders had been first revealed to Europe by the traveller Marco Polo in the 13th century. Not many years after Da Gama's discovery of the Cape route (1516), the Portuguese had penetrated to Canton, and by the middle of the 16th century (1542) had established relations with Japan, where, for a time, they exerted a great influence, and carried on a lucrative trade. When the Dutch reached the East they were not slow to follow in the footsteps of their rivals. Seven years after the foundation of the Company they sent ships to Japan, and continued to trade there every year, in spite of the violent opposition of the Portuguese. Finally they were allowed to set up a factory on Firando, an island to the west of Kiusiu, and this soon became one of the most profitable stations of the Company's trade.

In 1635 a certain William Verstegen, residing at Firando, sent a letter to Batavia stating that the Japanese reported that many miles to the eastward, in latitude 37½° North, there was "a very great country or island, rich without measure in gold and silver, and inhabited by civilised and friendly people." This was just the sort of report to excite the imaginations of those early traders, who were constantly tantalised by dreams of a new Mexico or Peru to be discovered in the Pacific. It was known that in 1620 the Spaniards had searched in vain for this golden island; but, undeterred by the former failure, Governor-General Van Diemen and his Council resolved to fit out an expedition to make the discovery. The scheme, through various domestic troubles, lay in abeyance for some years, but in 1639 two ships were fitted out for the adventure. Tasman's ship, the *Engel*, was one of the vessels chosen. The other was named the *Gracht* (*Canal*), and was under the command of an experienced sailor and pilot, Matthys H endrikszoon Quast, under whom Abel had sailed as mate in the *Banda* on the homeward voyage three years before. Quast was chief, and Tasman second in command. Tasman was now about 35 years old; he had been but six years in the Company's service, and had not only risen from the grade of a simple sailor to that of captain of a ship, but was now entrusted with the second place in a difficult and important enterprise. His rapid, promotion proves that Quast and the Colonial authorities had recognised in him high qualities as a seaman and a leader of men. The ships sailed from Batavia on 2nd June and made their way round the north of the Philippine Islands, keeping a northeasterly course until on 20th July they sighted some islands belonging to a group now known as the Bonin Archipelago. Thence they steered north-east, and then hack to the Japan coast searching for the land of gold. From this point they pushed out again into the great ocean further than any one before them, to a distance of some 2000 miles east from Japan. For two months longer they cruised backwards and forwards in those far northern seas, between 37½° and 46° north latitude, straining their eves in vain for some indication of the golden island. They were in a wretched condition. Many of the crew had died, and the number of sick increased daily. The remnant were worn out with the hardships of the voyage, and barely able to do the incessant pumping necessary to keep their leaky vessels afloat. Their provisions were running short, and there was still no faintest sign of land. Disappointed and dejected, the commanders and ships' council reluctantly resolved to give up a fruitless search. On the 25th October they turned their ships for Formosa to obtain refreshment for the sick, and to refit. Taking the coast of Japan on their way, they came to an anchor on the 24th November, before Fort Zealandia, on the island of Tayouwan or Formosa, then a Dutch possession. They had been nearly six months at sea, and out of a crew of ninety had lost nearly forty men. No further search was ever made for the wonderful island.

In the following year Tasman made another voyage to Japan, this time for the purposes of trade, as skipper of the fly-ship *Oostkappel* (*Eastchapel*). The fleet with which he sailed consisted of eleven ships, carrying freight valued at £525,000; The Oostkappel's cargo alone was worth £80,000. This gives us an idea of the value of the Japan trade. The Hollanders were now the only Europeans allowed to trade with the country. The Portuguese had for nearly a century carried on a most profitable trade, but their arrogance and intrigues, and above all the proselytising zeal of the Jesuit missionaries--who had made many thousand converts, and acquired an enormous influence--excited the jealousy and hostility of the Government. Christianity was suppressed: Foreigners were excluded from the Empire, and only allowed to trade with Firando and Nagasaki. In 1639 an insurrection led to a general massacre of the Christians, and the absolute expulsion of the Portuguese under pain of death.

The *Oostkappel* arrived at Firando on 25th August, 1640, and lay there for some three months. During her stay the Dutch got into serious trouble with the Japanese Government and were compelled to demolish their factory, which was too much like a fort to satisfy the susceptibilities of the Imperial Government. Mr. Lauts has given us the resolutions of the Council of the Dutch Factory at Firando in 1640. When the Imperial rescript arrived, Tasman, in virtue of his commission as captain of the *Oostkappel*, sat as a member of the Council, and signed its resolutions, The situation was most perilous, but Francis Caron, the president of the Council, returned the prudent answer: "All that His Imperial Majesty is pleased to command, we will punctually obey." Still the Dutch were slow in proceeding with the work of demolition, and it was not until another Imperial rescript arrived, threatening to put the members of the Council to death if the order was not instantly obeyed, that the great stone factory--which had cost the Dutch 100,000 guilders to build--was finally levelled to the ground. They were compelled to submit to the most vexatious restrictions, and to put up with countless humiliations in order to maintain their position. But the trade was too valuable to be lightly relinquished, and by their submission the Dutch alone of European nations for more than 200 years managed to retain trade relations with Japan, though living as the Japanese said "like frogs in a well," until in 1853 the American squadron under Commodore Perry broke in upon Japanese isolation and paved the way for that remarkable revolution, the latest development of which we have seen in the recent war between Japan and China.

In May, 1641, Tasman sailed from Batavia to take in a cargo at Lauwek, the capital of Cambodia, and then to proceed to Japan. The Cambodian Kingdom at that time extended over a great portion of south-eastern Further India, now Cochin China. Its capital, Lauwek, on the great river Cambodia, was one of the most important cities of the east; it was the centre of a great trade in furs, ivory, silk stuffs, and other merchandise, which were brought from the interior and from China and exported to Japan and other places. The Dutch, as the price of assistance given to the King in some of his wars, had a few years previously obtained leave to set up a factory at Lauwek, which was of great value to them in the Japan trade. For this factory Tasman sailed in his ship the Oostkappel, and in July came to an anchor in the Lauwek Roads. On his arrival he found the Dutch and Portuguese in violent conflict. A few days before a dispute had arisen between the crew of the Dutch fly-ship *Zaijer* arid the Portuguese, and this, through the overbearing arrogance of the latter, had grown into a fight, and had cost some of the Dutch their lives. The Directors of the factory had appealed to the King to punish the offenders, but the Portuguese having won him over by bribes were only sentenced to pay a fine. This blood-money the Dutch refused with contempt, and since neither by entreaty nor in any other way could they obtain a juster sentence, they resolved to exact satisfaction themselves. At this critical juncture Tasman made his appearance at La uwek, and as he lacked neither the courage nor the inclination to avenge the murder of his countrymen, he soon found an opportunity of inflicting an exemplary punishment on the enemy.[*1]

Since their expulsion from Japan the Portuguese had contrived to keep a share of the trade by importing their wares under the Cambodian flag. On the *Oostkappel's* arrival, a rich cargo of silks from Macao (the Portuguese settlement at the mouth of the Canton River) was being

24

transhipped into two junks flying the Cambodian flag in order to be sent to Japan. Tasman had express instructions to attack and make prizes of all Spanish, Portuguese, and other foreign ships not provided with free passes from the Dutch Company giving them permission to trade. He therefore rapidly discharged his cargo, loaded for Formosa, and then weighed anchor and cruised outside the river to look out for the Portuguese junks. A few days after leaving the river the junks hove in sight, and Tasman gave chase. He soon overhauled one of them, and after a sharp fight the junk surrendered, and her silks, worth 5500 dollars, were transferred to the *Oostkappel*. The other junk (with a cargo worth 5000 dollars), aided by the gathering darkness, succeeded in escaping, and Tasman, abandoning further pursuit, proceeded with his spoil to Formosa. His conduct in this matter did not, however, meet with the approval of the authorities at Batavia, arid Abel, for his alleged negligence in not capturing the second junk, was condemned to forfeit two months' wages. On leaving Formosa, the *Oostkappel* was overtaken by a violent storm. She lost her mainmast, and was so disabled that the ship's council judged it impossible to proceed with the voyage to Japan. The ship therefore made for Formosa, and after a most perilous voyage contrived to reach. Fort Zealandia. Here the cargo for Japan was transhipped to the *Zaijer*, and the *Oostkappel* was sufficiently repaired to be able to sail under jury rig with a cargo of silks for Batavia, where she arrived on 20th December.

Although Tasman, as we have said, was fined two months' wages for dereliction of duty in allowing the Portuguese junk to escape him, it would appear that this was but a necessary part of the rigid discipline of the Company, and involved no real disgrace. His voyage with Quast in search of the "golden island" had tested his qualities of hardihood and endurance; his voyages to Japan had proved his skill and resource in seamanship; his services in the Banda Sea, and his smart action at Lauwek (in spite of nominal blame) had shown his courage and capacity, and his zeal and determination as a stout upholder of the rights and privileges--not to say of the arrogant assumptions--of the Company. Van Diemen, ever on the watch for capable and resolute men who could further his plans for the extension of Dutch supremacy in the East, had recognised Abel's great qualities. This is plain from the important enterprises with which he was constantly entrusted. So little did his failure to capture the junk affect his standing, that within three or four months after the infliction of the fine the Governor-General offered him the conduct of an important mission, in which not only his resolution but his diplomatic skill would be put to proof. Amongst other countries in which the Dutch had early established themselves was the great island of Sumatra. They had soon elbowed out the Portuguese, and now had factories at Acheen, Djambi, and other places. The most important of these was at Palembang (not far from the coasts of Java.) This post commanded the pepper trade of the south of the island. The powerful Sultan of Palembang had long been on most friendly terms with the Dutch, but through the machinations of a Chinese named Bencki, who had fled from Batavia in debt to the Company, and had managed to ingratiate himself with the Sultan, these relations were seriously imperilled. The differences and misunderstandings which had arisen now threatened to end in war. It was with the view of bringing the Sultan to a better mind that Tasman was despatched to Palembang with a fleet of four vessels. He left Batavia on 23rd April, 1642, and two or three days later the little squadron cast anchor in the mouth of the river on which the Sultan's capital was situated. Here, by way of preliminary, Abel Jansz took possession of some junks loaded with pepper, and having transferred their cargoes to his own vessels, he sailed up the river to Palembang. His instructions were to do his best to arrange matters by friendly means before having recourse to hostile measures. He therefore sought an interview with the Sultan. To the surprise of the Dutch, the audience was not only granted, but the ambassador met with a most friendly reception. Abel showed himself a skilful diplomatist. He disabused the Sultan's mind of the prejudices instilled by the Chinaman, and dwelt on the good disposition of the government at Batavia. He showed the importance, not only to the Company but also to the kingdom of Palembang, of the maintenance of the trade and of the amicable relations hitherto existing. Finally he urged, in forcible terms, the mischief that would ensue from a war between the two hitherto friendly powers. It is perhaps doubtful whether the diplomatist's words would have been as convincing if they had not been supported by the tangible argument of a squadron of ships, commanded by a man who clearly was not to be trifled with. But, however that may be, the Sultan was completely won over, and without further hesitation renewed the treaty of friendship. Tasman's mission being thus successfully completed, he returned with his fleet to Batavia, carrying with him the obnoxious Chinaman, and was received by Van

Diemen and his Council with the warmest acknowledgments for his services in having extricated them from what had at one time threatened to. be a very serious trouble.

[*1) Voormeulen van Boekeren, p. 33.]

III.--THE GREAT DISCOVERY VOYAGES TO THE SOUTH-LAND, 1642-1644.

1. The Unknown South Land.

Tasman was now in his fortieth year. In ten years' wanderings and fightings in the service of the Company he had grown enured to hardships and danger. He was familiar with the great trade routes from Europe to India, with the intricacies of the waters of the Eastern Archipelago, and with the navigation of the Seas of China and Japan. He had sailed a thousand miles beyond the limits reached by any previous navigator into the unknown and mysterious regions of the cold and stormy North Pacific Ocean. In his many voyages he had proved himself a keen trader, a capable and daring seaman, a bold fighter, and an able commander. He was now ready to undertake the great adventure, the crowning achievement of his adventurous life--that voyage to the Great Southland, which, as a Dutch historian says, "must specially immortalise him; the expedition which must ever give him an honorable place amongst the greatest navigators and discoverers."

The Great Unknown Southern Continent--Terra Australis Incognita, or Nondum Cognita--had for ages been the dream of geographers. The ancient cosmographers had formulated a theory as to the existence of a huge continent in the south, which they considered necessary to balance the large continents in the northern hemisphere. The discovery of North and South America only lent fresh weight to this conjecture, and it was commonly supposed in the 16th and 17th centuries--and indeed was almost an article of faith--that below the Equator there was a huge continent which had still to be discovered and explored.

It was in 1513 that the Spaniard Vasco Nunez de Balboa first saw the Pacific from a mountain in Panama. Ferdinand Magellan was the first to enter it. Leaving Spain in 1519, with five small ships of from 130 to 60 tons, this heroic navigator felt his way through the Strait which bears his name, and crossing the great ocean, after months of suffering reached the Ladrones. He himself was killed at the Philippines, but one of his ships, the *Victoria*, with a handful of men, returned to Spain, after a voyage lasting three years, having been the first to circumnavigate the globe. Magellan voyage was prompted by the desire of Spain to find a way to the Moluccas on the west, with the object of disputing the claims of Portugal, and wresting from her the spice trade. With a similar object, the Spanish Viceroys of Mexico and Peru dispatched various expeditions to the Moluccas. In one of these voyages in 1528, Saavedra, sent out by Cortez, sighted New Guinea, which had previously been seen by the Portuguese. In 1564, the Philippines were colonised by the Spaniards. In another voyage, in 1568 Mendana discovered the Solomons, and brought to Peru such a glowing account of their wealth that in 1595 he was dispatched with a fleet to found a settlement there. He failed, however, to find the islands, and unsuccessfully attempted to plant a colony on Santa Cruz. Fernandoz do Cuiros, his pilot on the voyage, was firmly persuaded that here at last was the great Terra Australis. He petitioned the King of Spain to be allowed to colonise it, and in his memorial "it is soberly affirmed to be a terrestrial paradise for wealth and pleasure". He declares that the country abounds in fruit and animals, in silver and pearls, probably also in gold, and is nothing inferior to Guinea in the land of Negroes. In 1605 Cuiros set out from Peru with a powerful fleet, to settle a plantation in the southern paradise. On a large island which he discovered, and which he took to be part of the southern continent, and named Australia del Espiritu Santo--it is in fact one of the New Hebrides--he founded the short lived and unfortunate town of New Jerusalem. One of his companions, Louis Paz de Torres, separated from the fleet and steered westwards, sailing through the Strait which now bears his name, and skirting the south coast of New Guinea. The first Englishman to enter the Pacific was Sir Francis Drake. In his "Famous Voyage" in 1577 he stole through Magellan Strait, fell upon and plundered the Spanish settlements in Peru, and, following Magellans track across the South Sea, made the Moluccas, and returned to England laden with booty. In the latter part of the 16th and early part of the 17th centuries, several Dutch navigators accomplished similar circumnavigation. All these expeditions crossed the Pacific near the Equator, and though they discovered islands they threw no light on the problem of the Terra Australis. More important was the voyage of the Dutch navigators LeMaire and Schouten in 1616. They found a new passage into the South sea, between Tierra del Fuego and Staatenland. Sailing through the Strait of LeMaire, they reached the open ocean, doubled Cape Horn, and crossed the Pacific at a higher latitude than Magellan and Drake. Being so far to the south as 17° S latitude, they confidently expected to fall in with the Great South Land, but were constantly disappointed, finding nothing but a few islands. LeMaire's ships, on reaching Batavia after their long voyage, were seized and confiscated by his countryman Governor-General Cohen, for having come into the Indies in violation of the charter of monopoly of the Dutch Est India Company. This damped the ardour of explorers for many years, so much son that for nearly a century no Dutch navigator ventured again to attempt the circumnavigation of the globe.

These various expeditions had somewhat circumscribed the possible area within which the south land might be found. Still the old cartographers found the idea of a sea full of island so little in harmony with their prepossessions, that in the early part of the 17th C (even so late as 1640) they boldly drew on their maps of the world a huge Terra Australis Nondum Cognita. This was depicted as surrounding the South Pole, and occupying a very considerable portion of the Southern Hemisphere. In the South Atlantic the Promontorium Terrae Australis jutted northwards toward Africa. On the West only the narrow Straits of Magellan and LeMaire broke its continuity with South America and gave the sole means of passage into the South Sea. On the eastern side this continent of the mapmakers blocked all access to the Pacific. It extended in a solid but gradually narrowing mass from the pole up to the very Equator. In this respect the maps were a jumble, compounded of discoveries, actually made but imperfectly known, fitted onto a baseless theory. It is pretty certain that Portuguese ships sailing from the eastern archipelago had somewhere between 1512 and 1542 seen the northwest coast of Australia and that these discoveries were vaguely indicated on some of the early charts. They appeared on the cartographers maps as the land Beach, exceedingly rich in gold. New Guinea had been sighted by the Portuguese, Maneses in 1511, and again by the Spaniard Saavedra in 1528; therefor Nova Guinea appeared as the most northerly extension as the continent under the Equator--sometimes as an island separated by a narrow strait, sometimes as an integral part of the continent itself. Beyond New Guinea it is probable that the reported discovery by the Portuguese of certain vague and imperfectly known lands forming part of the coast of Australia justified the delineation of the north eastern shores of the continent. But from the point where information failed, imagination stepped in, boldly carrying the coastline from Queensland down in a south-easterly direction to Magellan Strait and Cape Horn, and filling the South Pacific with an imaginary continent.[*1]

When the Dutch had established themselves in the eastern Archipelago, their spirit of enterprise and adventure, and their ambition to win new realms for the Companies trade, were only stimulated by their unprecedented success. It became an object of ardent desire to the home directors, the Council of Seventeen, and to the successive Governors-General of the Indies, to explore the mystery of the Great Southland; if per chance they might there find a second Mexico or Peru, rich in Gold or Silver or new spice islands, to increased the profits of their trade, or, at the least, to discover a direct way from the eastern possessions, by the Great South Sea, to Peru and Chili, which would make it easy for them to harass and plunder the Spanish ships and the settlements of South America. It was in 1605--only three years after the foundation of the company--that the first attempt was made; and the object of this expedition was limited to the exploration of the regions lying to the east of the Banda islands. With this view, the *Duyfke* (*Little Dove* or *Darling*) sailed from Batavia in 1605, visited the island of Aru, sailed along the south coast of New Guinea and reached Cape Keer Weer, in 13° S latitude on the east side of the Gulf of Carpentaria--her captain thinking, however, that he was still on the west coast of New Guinea.

For a number of years the want of suitable vessels which could be spared from the needs of the east India settlements, and the hostilities in which they were constantly involved with their European rivals in the spice trade, coupled with thew necessity of consolidating their power in the Eastern Archipelago, prevented the Colonial authorities from engaging in distant adventures. The first Dutch discoveries on the west coast of Australia were not the result of design, but were accidental--or, at least, unpremeditated.

[*1) The prepossession in favour of a Southern Continent was inveterate in the 17th and 18th centuries. When Tasman made the west coast of New Zealand he was confident that at last he had discovered the west side of the long-sought Terra Australis Incognita So late as 1771, Alexander Dalrymple-- the Hydrographer to the Admiralty, and the jealous rival of Cook--published a collection of voyages to the South Sea with the express object of demonstrating the existence of a huge Southern Continent. The only part of the Pacific then unexplored was that lying between New Zealand and Magellan Strait. This gave nearly the area which, by elaborate calculation, Dalrymple showed was necessary to preserve the equilibrium of land between the northern and southern hemispheres. He therefore concluded that this space south of the Equator must be almost entirely solid land. Within four years of the publication of Dalrymple's work, Cook in his second voyage, by sailing over the site of the imaginary continent, finally dissipated the fable, and reduced the Terra Australis Incognita to the frozen mass within the Antarctic circle.]

When the Hollanders first made their way to the east Indies they naturally followed the old routes taken by their Portuguese predecessors and rivals. After rounding the Cape of Good Hope, they shaped their course, either inside or outside of Madagascar, and thence made their way as best they could--either north to India or east to Java. This rout had many disadvantages. Numerous rocks and islands, the positions of which were imperfectly known, lay in the track, and were a constant source of danger. The south-east Trade Winds drove the ships to the northward, and, as they got into the tropics, they met with light, variable, and baffling winds, which delayed them for long weeks, so that it was no uncommon thing for the outward voyage to last 13 months. Nor was the loss of time, and consequent damage to cargo the only evil. Scurvy--the scourge of all early voyages--produced by the long and exclusive use of salt diet, attacked the crews. Many died, and the survivors arrived at their destination broken down by sickness, and often short of provisions and water.

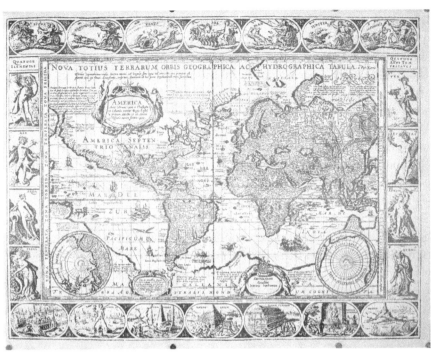

Nova Totius Orbis Geographica ac Hydrographica Tabula

(Peter Kærius [Pieter van den Keere, 1571-c.1647?])

Bad as the Madagascar route was, the Dutch, for more than 15 years, were unable to find a better. At last, however, in December, 1611, commander Hendrik Brouwer, who had sailed with two ships from Holland to the east, wrote to the Council of Seventeen reporting his arrival at Java. After leaving the Cape, he had run due east in about 36° S latitude for some 3000 miles. He had kept a strong westerly wind for 28 days, and had reached Batavia after a passage of less than seven months, having lost only two men from sickness. This was unprecedented; and he strongly advised that all outward bound ships should be ordered to take the south route, by which they might make sure of short passages--seeing that if they failed to get west winds in 36° S, they would be certain to do so if they ran to 40° or 44° S. Although the long distance run to the south seemed a disadvantage, it was largely compensated for by the gain of running down the easting in a high latitude. It was open sea all the way in this Great Southern Ocean, with none of the rocks and dangers which beset the northern route and the coolness of the weather was of great importance to the health of the crews.

In consequence of Brouwers report, seconded by the recommendation of Governor-General Cohen, the Directors ordered their outbound ships to take the new route. Rewards were offered for quick passages-- 150 Guilders for a passage under 9 months, 600 Guilders if they arrived within seven months. The superiority of the new route was soon apparent. Of three ships sailing at the same time from Holland in 1614, the *Hardt* took Brouwers route and reached Batavia in six months, while the two others by the Madagascar passage were 16 and 18 months in making the voyage. It was in running far east under the new sailing directions that in 1616 the ship *Eendragt (Concord)* first sighted the south land (the west coast of Australia) in 26° S latitude at Shark Bay; her captain Dirk Hartog landing on an island which still bears his name and putting up an inscribed metal plate, which remained there up to the early part of the present century. The voyage was not without danger, as an English ship, the *Tryal*, found to her cost; for, following the new Dutch route in 1621 she ran onto the Trial rocks in 20° S latitude and was totally wrecked, only a few of her crew succeeding in reaching Batavia in the boats.

From Hartog's ship, the new discovery received the name of Eendragt Land and in the next four or five years the captains of other ships on the same voyage sighted the west coast, amongst them Edel and Houtman, who in 1619 made the South Land in 32.5° S latitude--north of the present site of Perth--and sailed along it some hundreds of miles, giving it the name of Edel Land, and also naming Houtmans Abrolhos.

Instructions were issued by the directors in 1620 and 1621 that outward bound ships leaving the Cape should keep an east course between 30° and 40° S latitude for 4000 miles, or until they should sight the New South Land of the Eendragt'. With our modern notions these instructions appear extraordinary, but in the then existing state of navigation they were practical and well judged. The appliances at the command of ships captains in those days were very imperfect. Without the sextant or the chronometer there was the greatest difficulty in determining the ships position. It is true that they could find the latitude by the cross-staff with reasonable accuracy, but they had no means of finding the longitude except by the rude process of dead reckoning by the log. They had no reliable charts, and had to depend very largely on their own personal experience of former voyages or on the advice of pilots who had sailed the seas before. It was therefor no uncommon thing at the end of a long voyage for the captain to find himself some hundreds of miles out of his reckoning--sometimes even as much as 400 or 600 miles. Thus Brouwer, in the voyage above mentioned--made Sumatra, when according to his estimated position on the chart he was still 320 miles to the westward of the island. The object of the new instructions was, therefore, to enable the ships to ascertain their position after the long run to the east. When they made the South Land they ran north along the coast until they reached the known point of Eendragt Land in 25° or 26° S latitude. From this they took a new departure, and by steering an N.N.W.

Course they could make pretty sure of striking the south coast of Java. The new plan lead to several ships sighting various parts of the west coast of Australia in the course of the next 6 or 7 years. Amongst others, the dispatch *Leeuwin* (*Lioness*), in 1622 doubled the Cape to which she gave her name. Even by the new route the voyage to the Indies was often very protracted, the *Leeuwin* for instance, taking 13 months to reach Batavia. There was also the danger of overshooting the mark, as Pieter Nuyts found (1627) when in the *Gulde Zeepart* (*Golden Seahorse*) he found himself at the islands of St. Peter and St. Francis at the head of the Great Australian Bight, and had to coast back some hundreds of miles until he could round Cape Leeuwin.

The new discoveries quickly attracted quickly the attention and interest not only of the Colonial Government but of the Home Directors, and were a frequent subject of correspondence between the Council of Seventeen and their Governors-General. Cohen respecting the discovery of a great land situate to the south of Java reported by the ship *Eendragt*, Commanders Houtman, Edel, and others, recommending that ships should be sent to examine it and report on its inhabitants and resources, and the opening it might offer for profitable trade; and also to try to find a passage eastward into the Great South Sea. Accordingly in the next few years several attempts at systematic exploration were made, but with little success. The only result was the discovery by the ships *Pera* and *Arnhem*, in 1623, of a portion of the north coast of Australia (now part of the Northern Territory of South Australia), which was named Arnhem Land and the naming of the Golf of Carpenteria, after the Governor-General Carpentier.

One further addition to the knowledge of these coasts was made by DeVitt, whose ship, the *Vianen*, leaving the East Indies in January

1628, in the north-west monsoon, was driven onto the north west coast of Australia, about the Kimberly district, and who named the country DeVitt Land.

The total result of these various discoveries and explorations was that the coast of Australia, from Cape York on the North to the center of the Great Australian Bight on the south, had been traced more or less continuously by Dutch ships in the twelve years between 1616 and 1628. This coast was now called by the Dutch "The Known South Land" to differentiate it from those unexplored and supposititious regions for which, with practical sense they retained the old appellation of "The unknown South Land." Down to very recent times, the names of these early Dutch discoveries were retained on the maps of Western Australia. Half a century ago, when across the center of Australia was written the simple word "Unexplored," almost the only names appearing on the western coast were those given two hundred years before by the captains of the ships of the Dutch East India Company in the early years of the 17th C. Beginning with Nuyts Land in the great Australian Bight, and going north, we had Leeuwin Land, Edel Land, Eendragt Land, DeVitt Land, and Arnhem land. A few names still remain as evidence of the Dutch discoveries--Cape Leeuwin, Houtmans Abrolhos, Dirk Hartog's Island, and the Gulf of Carpentaria.

Such was the state of Dutch knowledge of Australia when Antony van Diemen became Governor-General of the Dutch Indies, in the year 1636. Van Diemen was one of the most notable of the many notable men who served the east India Company in the early years of its power. Being involved in debt, he had gone to the Indies, either to escape his creditors or to retrieve his fortunes. He showed so much capacity that he was appointed Secretary to Governor-General Coen. From this time his rise was rapid. In 1626 he became one of the Councillors of the Indies, and, after important services, he was appointed Governor-General, in 1636.[*1]

He came to his government at a time when the Dutch power had been so firmly consolidated by Coen, Carpentier, Brouwer, and others of his predecessors in office, that the Dutch were undisputed masters of the Eastern Archipelago, and had a virtual monopoly of the trade. Free from the difficulties with the native powers, and foreign rivals, which had embarrassed his predecessors, he had the leisure and the means to prosecute new enterprises. His zeal for discoveries which might bring increased wealth and power to his company was unbounded, and as shown not only by his frequent dispatches on the subject top the Council of Seventeen in Holland, but by the expeditions, which he planned and sent out during the term of his nine years government.

It will be observed that the first attempts at exploration from the Dutch East India Settlements were directed to the regions east of the Banda Sea, and had for their chief object the exploration of New Guinea, and especially the determination of the question whether New Guinea and the known South Land formed one continent, or whether there was a strait between them by which access could be gained to the Great South Sea. It was to the solution of this problem that Van Diemen first applied himself in the very year in which he received his appointment as Governor-General, ignorant of the fact that the Spaniard Torres had already solved the problem by sailing through the strait that now bears his name, in the year 1606.[*1]

[*1) Du Bois: *Vies des Gouverneurs Généraux.*]

In the year 1636 Van Diemen dispatched two ships from Banda under the command of Captain Gerrit Thomasz Pool, with instructions to proceed along the south coast of New Guinea. If, contrary to all expectation, a strait was found between New Guinea and the South Land, Pool was to sail through it and trace, if possible, the east coast of the Known South Land, circumnavigating it and returning home along Nuyts Land and Eendragt Land. If, however, as seemed most probable, New Guinea was joined to the Known South Land, he was to sail along the northern and western coast of Australia as far south as Houtmans Abrolhos, searching all the way for any possible passage to the Pacific. More particularly was he to search the more northerly parts, as it was presumed that a strait was more likely to be found in that quarter than further south, where the South Land was presumably much wider. If Pool with some of his crew had not been murdered by the savages of New Guinea, it is possible that he might have assailed through the strait already traversed by Torres, and have anticipated Captain Cook in the discovery of New South Wales. As it happened, however, the ships returned without having discovered anything of importance. In the same year Van Diemen planned the expedition to search for the supposed "golden island", east of Japan, which three years later was undertaken by Quast and Tasman, with the result we have already seen.

2. The Planning of the Great Discovery Voyage

Governor Van Diemen's heart was now set on a complete exploration of the Unknown South Land, in which he hoped to discover a new Peru, rich in silver and gold, or at the least fertile countries inhabited by civilised people, in which might be found new and as yet undreamed of commodities to bring fresh wealth into the already overflowing coffers of the East India Company. For some years domestic troubles and the want of suitable ships delayed the execution of his plans; but in the year 1641 he writes to the Council of seventeen:--"We are very desirous to make discovery of the South Land. The fly-ship *Zeehaen* was intended for this service, but through the strange delay of the ships from Persia and Suratte we were compelled to employ this same *Zeehaen* for the last voyage to Taiwan and Japan. Moreover, we have kept here in the harbour idle, as much to his vexation as to our own, the renowned pilot Frans Visscher, whom we intend to employ for the discovery of the South Land; however, this shall, as we hope, be effected once for all".

[*1) The discovery of Torres remained unknown until the English took Manilla in 1762, and discovered in the Archives a copy of Torres' original letter to the King of Spain. *See* Major: *Early Voyages.*]

This same Frans Jacobszoon, *alias* Visscher, took an important part as the adviser of the Governor-General Van Diemen in his plans for the projected voyage of discovery. Visscher was a native of Flushing, and had been for many years in the service of the company. He had repeatedly made the outward and homeward voyages. In 1623, as mate of the ship *Hope*, he had sailed around the world in the celebrated Nassau fleet, under the command of L'Hermite and Schapenham. He had traded in the east for many years, chiefly in the Japan trade, and was thoroughly acquainted with the coast of Tonquin, Chine and Formosa. In those days, when navigation had not been reduced to a science, and charts were either wanting or not to be depended on, the Dutch captains in the uncharted seas had to place their chief reliance for safe and prosperous voyages on the personal experience of those officers and seamen who in former voyages had gained a knowledge of the coasts and rocks, the currents, and the winds of the seas they were traversing. These pilots, for the most part, were jealous of their knowledge, and indisposed to make it public, notwithstanding the repeated complaints and injunctions of the company. Amongst these pilots, Visscher, from his long and varied experience, and from his skill and capacity, was one of the most renowned. His knowledge and experience were freely placed at the disposal of the company, as is often made matter of honourable mention in the despatches of the Governor-General. He had made charts of the coasts and islands of the China Seas, of Formosa, the Piscadores, and Japan, and is continually referred to as one of the best chart-makers of his time. It was this man that van Diemen consulted on the projected expedition, and, as we have seen, for this purpose he detained him-very much to Visschers chagrin in these stirring times-for nine months in idleness in Batavia, for the benefit of his advice.

In January, 1642, Visscher wrote a report to the Governor-General on the proposed discovery of the Unknown South Land. The report is a masterly document, and gives us a high idea not only of Visschers practical ability and knowledge as a seaman, but also of his sagacity and sound judgment. The old pilot wastes no words on fanciful speculations about the unknown South Land. He goes straight to the point, states the conditions necessary for success, discusses possible difficulties, and, in short and concise terms, lays down a clearly defined and carefully thought out scheme--or rather choice of schemes--for exploring both the Unknown and Known South Lands, and, indeed, for obtaining a knowledge of the whole southern world.

The report begins with a recommendation that the expedition should leave Batavia in August, when they would have the most favourable winds, and have the whole of the summer before them, with long days and good weather. From Batavia the ships should first proceed to Mauritius, then a Dutch possession. As the expedition was intended to go to the east, this, at first sight, seems a strange recommendation. But there were good grounds for the advice. Visscher, as we shall see, had certain reasons for wishing to make the point of departure as far to the west as possible. Mauritius, moreover, was easily reached with the south-east trades, and when there the ships would have run down nearly a thousand miles of their southing, and would have a comparatively short distance to run to the south before reaching the region of the westerly winds, on which they must depend for success. Moreover, at Mauritius, and this is the only reason explicitly stated in the report, they could conveniently take in wood, water, and other supplies necessary for the voyage.

Leaving Mauritius early in October, the ships were to get away south as quickly as possible to 51° or 54° south latitude, or until they fell in with land. From this point they should run due east upon the same latitude to the longitude of the east end of New Guinea, and then steer a course north by west until they got new Guinea on board; or else they might run further to the east to the supposed longitude of the Solomon Islands--or perhaps 500 or 700 miles beyond--then steer north-explore those islands--where, according to all accounts, they would find many things worth their trouble--and return by the north coast of New Guinea to Banda or Amboyna.

But Visscher had an alternative scheme, or rather a combination of two schemes, by which a much more complete exploration could be made. If an exploring expedition was fitted out in Holland, the ships might make the Cape of Good Hope, and thence sail south to latitude 54° S., or make Rio de Janeiro, and begin from the east side of Staaten Land, near Cape Horn; in either case running east to the longitude of the Solomon islands, and making the homeward voyage as before. Such a voyage would give a knowledge of the whole Southern Ocean from Cape Horn to the Solomon Islands. Of course if land was met with the plans would be modified, but Visscher apparently had not much faith in the common belief in a huge southern continent, at least in the Atlantic and Indian oceans. About the South Pacific he was more doubtful. Here the difficulty of exploration would be greater. The strong westerly winds prevailing in the latitude of Cape Horn would make it impossible for any ship to make the voyage to the west in a high latitude; but if the Dutch had a settlement in Chili, the expedition might start from there and run up into the tropics with the south-east trades to latitudes 12* or 15° S., crossing the Pacific in that latitude until it made the Solomons. If they could only be sure of getting refreshment at the Solomon Islands this would be an excellent plan, for they could then sail south from the Solomons, and getting into westerly winds run back east to the Strait of Le Maire and Cape Horn.

By the accomplishment of these two voyages, says Visscher, "You will be able to explore the southern portion of the world round about the whole globe, and find out what is there; whether it be land or sea or icebergs--whatever God has ordained to be there". The old pilots views as to the South Land, and the best means to search for it, show that he was in advance of his time, and free from many of the traditional prepossessions then common amongst navigators and geographers. If the Council of Seventeen could only have been induced to enter into Visscher's plans, the riddle of the South Land might have been solved in the 17th C., and the discoveries of Captain Cook anticipated by more than one hundred and twenty years.

These large schemes were beyond the province of the East India Government, but the plan Visscher had sketched for the expedition from Batavia was adopted in its entirety. Van Diemen in his despatches describes the voyage as having been projected on the advice of Visscher. The resolution of the Governor-General and Council decreeing the expedition is dated 1st August, 1642. It begins by stating the great desire of both the colonial and home governments for the exploration of southern and eastern lands, with the hope of opening up important areas for trade, or at least finding a more convenient way to the rich countries already known in South America. The Governor then states that he has consulted divers persons of approved judgement in such matters, and especially the renowned and most experienced pilot Frans Jacobsz Visscher, as to the explorations and the bets way to accomplish them, and in accordance with their written opinions has decided to dispatch for the discovery of these apparently rich countries two ships**[*1]**, the *Heemskerck*, with a crew of sixty men, and the fly-ship *Zeehaen (Cormorant)*, with a crew of fifty. The expedition to be under the command of the Hon. Abel Tasman, who is very eager to make the exploration; with him are to be associated the said Pilot-Major Visscher and other capable officers.

[*1) The *Heemskerck* was a jagt or small ship, perhaps 20 tons. The *Zeehaen* was a fluit or fly-boat, a vessel of light draught, built for quick sailing; she was smaller than the *Heemskerck*.]

The ships were ready for sea. The *Heemskerck* had for skipper Ide Tjerxszoon, the *Zeehaen* Gerrit Janszoon. Tasman as commander and Visscher as pilot-major were on board the *Heemskerck*, Gilsemans the merchant or super-cargo on the *Zeehaen*. In all Dutch discovery and trading expeditions the merchant or supercargo was an important personage. He had the direction of the commercial part--which in the Company's voyages was the chief part of the undertaking--and consequently had a large voice in the direction of the expedition. Gilsemans is spoken of as having a competent knowledge of navigation and as being also a skilful draftsman, and it doubtless to his capable pencil that we owe the vigorous sketches which illustrate the original journal of the voyage.

The instructions to Tasman were printed by Swart in 1859, and are entitled "Instructions for the Captain-Commander Abel Janszoon Tasman, the Pilot-Major Franchoys Jacobsz Visscher, and the Council on the ship *Heemskerck* and fly-boat the *Zeehaen*, destined for the exploration of the Unknown and Discovered South Land, the South-Eastern Coast of New-Guinea, with the Islands lying round about". They begin with an elaborate exordium recounting the priceless riches, profitable commerce, useful traffic, excellent dominion, great might and power which the kings of Castile and Portugal had brought to their crowns by the discovery of America by Columbus and of the Cape route to the Indies by Vasco de Gama; likewise what uncounted blind heathen had thus come to the wholesome light of the Christian religion. Yet hitherto no serious attempt had been made by any Christian king, prince, or republic to explore the still unknown part of the globe situated in the south, which might be supposed to be as great as either the old or the new world, and might with good reason be expected to contain many excellent and fruitful countries, and also lands as rich in mines or precious metals as the gold and silver provinces of Peru, Chili or Sofala. No European colony was so suitable for the starting-point of such an expedition as the town of Batavia, situated in the centre of the known and unknown East India; therefore the Governor and Council of India had resolved to take the discovery in hand, and to dispatch for that service the ships *Heemskerck* and *Zeehaen*.

The instructions then prescribe the course which the vessels are to take, following exactly the recommendations of Visschers report, except that, if the ships council for any sufficient reason thought it best, they might vary the route by making the east end of the known South Land, or the islands of St. Peter and St. Francis on the Great Australian Bight, and then sailing due north along the coast, (which it was presumed would turn here to the north) and try to discover a passage between it and new Guinea. However, this was not recommended; the course advised being to keep on south latitude 48° to 54° until 400 to 800 miles east of the supposed longitude of the Solomon Islands, so as to be assured there was a way through from the Indies to the South Pacific which would give a short route to Chili.

Minute directions are given for the survey and description of lands discovered; observations of winds, currents, and weather; precautions to be taken in navigation; discipline and rations of the crews; care in conciliating the natives and avoiding any injury to them; precautions to be observed against possible treachery when landing from boats; and injunctions to obtain information as to the resources of the countries visited, and the possibilities of trade with them.

It must be remembered that this, like other Dutch expeditions, was essentially commercial. It was no scientific or adventurous thirst for discovery that prompted these old Dutchmen, but plain practical business and the hope of profit for the Company. The merchant to whom was entrusted the management of the commercial venture had a large voice in the direction of the expedition. Consequently the instructions are specially precise in their injunctions to enter in the journal full particulars of the productions of the countries, what sort of goods the people had for trade, and what they would take in exchange. For this purpose the ships were laden with a great variety of articles of merchandise. Gold and silver were specially to be sought for but, says the Governor-General with cynical candour, "Keep them ignorant of the value of the same, appear as if you were not greedy for them; and if gold or silver is offered in any barter, you must feign that you do not value those metals, showing them copper, zinc, or lead, as if those minerals were of more value with us."

Tasman was to hoist his flag on the *Heemskerck* as commander of the expedition, and was to preside in the ships council, consisting of skippers of the two ships, Pilot-Major Visscher, the chief mates, and the two merchants. The commander had a deliberative and a casting vote. In the administration of justice the boatswains were also to be summoned and to have votes. But in all matters which concerned navigation, such as courses to be steered and the discovery of lands, the Pilot-Major was to have two votes, and his advice to be held in proper respect, seeing that the voyage had been projected on his advice and information. In these matters too, the second mates were to have votes.

In case of Tasman's death the skipper of the *Heemskerk*, Ide Tjerexszoon, was to succeed to the command.

The instructions conclude:--"We command you to the blessing of the Almighty, whom we pray to endue you with manly courage for the accomplishment of the proposed discoveries, and to bring you back in safety, to the increase of His glory, the reputation of the fatherland, the service of the company, and your own immortal honour".

They are dated Fort Batavia, 13th August, 1642, and signed by the Governor-General and his Council--Van der Lyn, Maetzuycker, Schouten, Sweers, Witsen, and Boreel.

3. The Voyage of 1642.

The next day (14th August) the ships sailed from Batavia, and on this day Tasman's journal begins as follows:--"Journal or description by me, Abel Jansz Tasman, of a voyage made from the Town of Batavia, in the East Indies, for the discovery of the Unknown Southland, in the year Anno 1642, the 14th August. May it please Almighty God to grant His blessing thereto! Amen".

Sailing through the Sunda straight, the ships carried the south-east trades with them to Mauritius, where they arrived 5th September, after an exceptionally quick passage of 22 days. An entry in Tasman's journal shows us how hopelessly abroad the best sailors in those days were in regard to longitude. He says, "By our reckoning we were still 200 miles to the east of Mauritius when we saw it". And he mentions the arrival at the same time of another ship, the *Arent*, outward bound, which had made the island of Rodrigues in the belief that it was Mauritius, because it lay in nearly the same latitude, though 300 miles to the eastward.

They had other difficulties to contend with. A letter from Van der Stael, the Dutch commandant at Mauritius, to the Governor-General at Batavia, states that the ships arrived in very bad condition, and wanting almost everything. The Zeehaen was partly rotten, and in need of extensive repairs. Both ships were leaky, their rigging was old and weak, their yards and other spars frequently giving way. To refit the ships, caulk the seams throughout, strengthen the rigging, cut and ship spare spars, took the crews nearly a month. Meantime they took in supplies of water, firewood, and other stores; and added to their stock of provisions by shooting wild hogs, wild goats, and other game abounding in the woods. Van der Stel gave to Tasman journals and maps relating to the Solomon Islands, and vocabularies of the languages of those islands and of New Guinea. The ships were ready for sea on 4th October, but through contrary winds, they could not get out of the harbour of Fort Fredrik Hendrik until the 8th. Taking a departure from the south end of Mauritius[*1], Tasman stood to the southward, getting variable winds to 31° or 32° S, when he came into the westerly winds. Passing far to the west of St. Pauls and Amsterdam, and between those islands and Kerguelen, he came, in 43° S, on floating seaweed and other indications of land. The ships council was called together, and it was resolved to keep a man constantly on the look-out at the masthead, and to offer as a reward to whoever should first see land three reals of eight and a mug of arrack. On 29th October, three weeks out, he made 46° S latitude, and, meeting with strong gales and fogs, thought it too dangerous to keep a southerly course for fear of falling in with land. The course was therefore changed to nearly east. On 6th November, four weeks out, he reached his highest latitude, 49° 4' S, seeing many indications of land, which kept him anxious.

The Pilot-Major now delivered to Tasman an elaborate paper, in which he carefully discussed the future course of the voyage. He proposed that they should fall off to 44° S. latitude until they had passed the 150th meridian[*2], when he judged that if they had not made the Southern Continent they would be in open sea. Then they should fall off to 40° S., and sail east to 220° longitude (about 160° W. according to our reckoning), which he judged would bring them well to the eastward of the Solomons, and enable them to make these islands with the south-east trades-as indeed it would, seeing that this would be about 15° east of the true position of the Solomons.

This resolution was communicated to the *Zeehaen* by enclosing the paper in a wooden case, and floating it astern by a long-line for the *Zeehaen* to pick up. The councils of both ships having given their approval, the course was altered accordingly, and on 18th November they passed the longitude of Nuyts Land (Great Australian Bight), the furthest known extension of the discovered South Land. Here they had heavy westerly gales, and gradually fell off to lat. 42° 25', when on the 24th November, they sighted their first land, which they called Antony van Diemen's Land, after the Governor-General.

[*1) AS might be expected, Tasman's longitudes are very inexact. They are reckoned east from the meridian of the Peak of Teneriffe. His longitude for the south point of Mauritius, when reduced to the meridian of Greenwichm is 3° 33' easterly of the true longitude. Similarly, that of Batavia is 4° 23' too easterly.]

[*2) About 130° wast of Greenwich--nearly the longitude of the head of the Great Australian Bight.]

This landfall was somewhere to the north of Point Hibbs, on the West Coast of Tasmania, probably near the entrance of Macquarie Harbour-- Mounts Heemskerck and Zeehaen[*1] being noticeable objects to the north-east. After standing off for the night, the ships next day made the land again, approaching within one Dutch mile (i.e. four English miles) of Point Hibbs. By carefully comparing reckonings the longitude was fixed at 163° 50'[*2], and a new departure taken. The wind now came easterly with thick weather, so that they could not see the land. Rounding South West Cape they got the wind from the north, and sailed along the south coast. Tasman named the outlying islands and some peaks on the broken coast, which he mistook for islands, after members of the council of India--Wit, Maatsuyker, Sweers, and Boreel. Passing between Pedra Branca and the main, and rounding the Friars (which he called Boreel Islands), south of Bruni, Tasman stood up for Adventure Bay, but was caught in a violent north-west gale, which drove the ships out to sea. From this incident the bay received its well known name of Storm Bay. Rounding Tasman's Island on the 1st December, he came to an anchor off what is now known as Blackman's Bay, but, which Tasman called Fredrik Hendrik Bay, in honour of the Stadtholder of the United Provinces. His anchorage was off Green Island, near Cape Frederik Henry on Forestier's Peninsula. Next day Pilot-Major Visscher was sent in the *Zeehaen's* boat through the Narrows to explore Frederik Hendrik (or Blackman's) Bay. On the 3rd, Tasman with two boats made for a little bay, now known as Prince of Wales Bay[*3], but the wind was so stiff from the south-east that the *Zeehaen's* launch with Visscher and Gilsemans on board had to run back to the ship. The *Heemskerck's* longboat with Tasman on board made the bay, but the surf was too high to allow of landing. The carpenter therefore swam through the surf, and planting the Prince's flag on shore, took formal possession of the newly discovered country.

On the 4th December Tasman weighed anchor, intending to sail northwards along the coast and take in water; the wind, however, was unfavourable, blowing from the north-west, and being unable to hold the land aboard, the ship's council resolved to stand away to the east. After naming Maria Island, Schouten Island, and Van der Lyn Island (Freycinet Peninsula), he took his departure from "a high round mountain"--probably St. Patrick's head, or St. Paul's dome[*1].

[*1) These mountains were so named by Flinders when he made the first circumnavigation of Tasmania in the *Norfolk* in 1798.]

[*2) East from Teneriffe.]

[*3) Mr. Gell thinks that this Prince of wales Bay is the Frederik Hendrick Bay of Tasman.]

Steering due east from the coast of Antony Van Diemen's Land, after nine days he sighted land again (13th December). This was the west coast of the South Island of New Zealand, to the south of Cook's strait.

In an interesting paper by Dr. T. M. Hocken, of Dunedin, on Tasman's discoveries in New Zealand, it is stated that "the great high land" that Tasman first saw is situated between Hokitika and Okarito. Further north the low point described in the journal is Cook's Cape Foulwind, with its outlying rocks, the Steeples, near Westport. North of this the Karamea Bight, and the "furthermost point, which stood out so boldly that we had no doubt that it was the extreme point", is Cook's Cape Farewell.

Coasting north-eastwards he made a bay on the north coast of the South Island, where he anchored. Here the Maori's in their war canoes attacked one of the *Zeehaen's* boats, killed three of the crew, and mortally wounded a fourth man. Tasman gave this bay the name of Moordenaars (or massacre) Bay. He says "This is the second land we have discovered; we have given it the name of the Staaten Land in honour of Their Mighty Highnesses the States General, and also because it may be that this land is joined to Staaten Land (near Cape Horn), but this is uncertain. It appears to be a very fine country. Believing that this is the main continent of the Unknown Southland, we have given this strait the name of Abel Tasman's Passage, as he has been the first to sail through it".[*2]

Massacre Bay is near the western entrance of Cook's Strait; it is now called Golden Bay, and the scene of the tragedy, according to Dr. Hocken, lies close to Parapara.

Although Tasman noted a south-east current and suspected that there must be a passage, the weather was so bad that he did not stay to look for it; if he had done so he would have sailed through Cook's Strait and corrected his idea that he had found the great Southern Continent. However, he sailed north along the west coast of the North Island and sighted the Three Kings Islands, on which they would have landed to get fresh water, but were deterred by seeing thirty or forty men of uncommon stature who showed themselves in a threatening attitude. He did not land in New Zealand, partly on account of bad weather and partly owing to the hostile attitude of the Maoris. After rounding the north of New Zealand he steered north-east after consultation with the ships council, and found a great swell from the south-east, which must have made him doubt the existence of the Great Southern Continent. It did indeed assure him that here was a clear passage to Batavia to Chili. Still holding a north-east course, on 21st January he came to several islands, to which he gave the names of Amsterdam, Middelburg, and Rotterdam, now known as Tongataboo, Eooa, and Annamooka, part of the Tonga or Friendly Group.

[*1] * Tasman's longitudes, reduced to the meridian of Greenwich, are for Point Hibbs, 147° 11'; for the anchorage off Green Island, 150° 51'. The true longitudes are 145° 15' and 148° 1' respectively. The first shows an error of 1° 56', the second an error of 2° 50', thus making Tasmania too broad by nearly one whole degree of longitude.
In the Papers and Proceedings of the Royal Society of Tasmania for 1890, is a paper by the present writer, in which the localities mentioned by Tasman in his journal are identified and described.]

[*2] The English Admiralty has lately given to the sea between Australia And New Zealand the name of the *Tasman Sea*.]

He was very hospitably received by the natives, and after a few days' stay he weighed anchor (1st February) and after discovering Willems' Shoals, south-east of Fiji, by the advice of Visscher and the council he stood north by west to 5° or 6° S. latitude, and then west for New Guinea. He sailed along the north coast of New Guinea, and arrived at Batavia on 15th June 1643, after an absence of ten months, during which he had lost ten men by sickness, besides the four men killed by the Maoris. His journal concludes thus: "God be praised and thanked for a safe voyage! Amen".

4. The Voyage of 1644.

Tasman had not, as Van Diemen had hoped, discovered any rich gold or silver mines, or indeed any rich trade for the Company, but he had circumnavigated New Holland, or, as he called it on the chart, "Compagnies Nieuw Nederlandt", and had found a clear way to Chili, which opened up a good prospect for trade, or at least for great spoil to be come at from the Spanish settlements in South America. From this last Governor-General Van Diemen hoped much. On 4th January,

1644, he wrote to the Home Directory that he contemplated fitting out a fleet in September to open up a Chili trade and to plunder the Spaniards in Peru. He also intended to send two or three ships to make an examination of the newly discovered South Land, which Tasman had found not possible. For he hoped that such great countries must contain much that would be profitable for the Company, and especially gold and silver mines, as in Peru, Chili, and Japan. But, in the meantime, it would much facilitate the attempts on Chili and Peru if a shorter passage could be found between New Guinea and the Known South Land.

This, the Governor-General announced, was to be immediately undertaken by two ships and a smaller vessel under the same commanders as before, viz.-Commander Tasman and Pilot-Major Frans Visscher; Gilsemans was again to be merchant or supercargo.

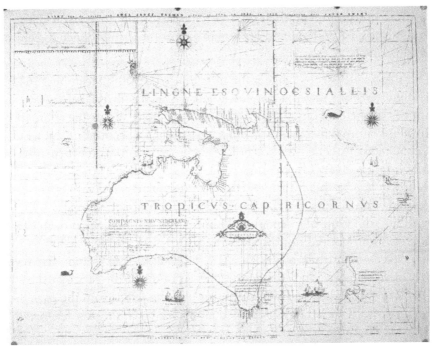

Map of the Voyages of Abel Tasman in 1642 and 1644.

Jacob Swart's colour facsimile, 1860.

On the 13th January, 1644, by resolution of the Governor-general in Council, the ships *Limmen* and *Zeemeeuw* (*Sea Gull*), with the little tender *Braek* (*Setter*) carrying only 14 men, were commissioned for the work.

They carried a compliment of 111 hands, and were provisioned for a eight months. On 29th January the instructions for the voyage were drawn up and signed. They were printed in England by Mr. Major in 1859.[*1] They contain a most interesting and valuable summary of former Dutch voyages in the South land. The vessels were to coast along the south and west coasts of New Guinea to the furthest discovery in 17° S. latitude (i.e. in the Gulf of Carpentaria) and endeavour to find a strait or passage into the South sea. If a strait was found, which might be known by the south-east swell through it, they were to sail along it and thence as far to the south-east as the new Van Diemens Land. From thence they were to make the islands of St. Peter and St. Francis, and run along the coast of the Known South Land to De Wit Land, in 22° S. latitude, when the known South Land would be circumnavigated and found to be the largest island in the globe. But if, as was to be presumed, New Guinea was joined to the South Land, forming one continent, then they were to run along the coast to 28° S. to the land of Eendragt and Houtman's Abrolhos, and thence to return to Batavia.

The ships sailed from Batavia the next day, (the 30th December, 1644). The journals of the voyage are lost, and we have only the briefest notices of the expedition[*2]. But Tasman's chart shows the route of the ships. For some reason or other, probably on account of the wind, Tasman and Visscher did not follow the instructions exactly. Instead of sailing first to New Guinea they made a strait course to the Land of Eendragt. From there Tasman coasted northwards, and carefully charted, with soundings, the west and north coasts of Australia, including the Gulf of Carpentaria. He actually got into the mouth of Torres Strait, but did not discover the passage. Probably he was deterred from further examination by the multitude of islands and reefs that block the way, and was, moreover, ignorant of the fact that the Spaniard Torres had in 1606 sailed through the strait from the east. Failing to find the strait he returned along the coast of New Guinea to Batavia, where he arrived in August, 1644.

[*1) Early voyages to Terra Australis.--Hakluyt Society, 1859.]

[*2) N. Witsen : "Noord en Oost Tartarye," translated by R. H. Major, in "Early Voyages to Terra Australis," pp. 91-98. The journal has been sought for in vain both in Holland and at Batavia, especially by Messrs. Van der Chijs and Norman in 1862.]

Van Diemen in his dispatch to the Home Directory, the Council of Seventeen, (23rd December, 1644), reports the result of the voyage, and expresses his disappointment and discontent that the expedition had not discovered a strait between New Guinea and the Known South Land, but only a great bay or Gulf, and also that they had done nothing but sail along the coasts, and had gained no knowledge of the country and its productions, alleging as a reason that they were not strong enough to venture to land in face of the savages. This was very disappointing, since discoveries were of little use unless the country was explored at the same time. "For it is certain that as long as we merely run along the coasts and shores we shall very slowly open up anything profitable, it being well known to everybody that the coast people are ordinarily poor, miserable, and evil disposed; therefore, we must go inland". (Letter: 29 Nov.) Yet, he says, Tasman in his two voyages had circumnavigated the hitherto Unknown South Land, which was calculated to have an extent of 8000 miles of coast; and it was very improbable that in so great a country, with such a variety of climates, there should not be found something of great importance and profit for the company. There were also the great northern lands of America, which had been made accessible by the new discoveries, and every opportunity would be taken to explore them from time to time by vigilant and courageous persons; "for", says Van Diemen, "the discovery of new countries is not work for everyone". "God grant", he concludes, "that in either one or the other (i.e., in the North America or the South Land) may be found a rich silver or gold mine, to the satisfaction of those engaged in the venture, and to the honour of the finders".

It is plain that Van Diemen was dissatisfied with Tasman. He had looked for immediate results in the extension of trade, or at least for the finding of the New Guinea strait, and, disappointed in this, he could not appreciate the importance of the discoveries from a geographical standpoint.

Tasman's services were recognised somewhat grudgingly. By resolution of the Governor-General and Council (4th October, 1644) his salary was raised to 100 florins (£9.6.8) per month, and the reasons are stated in measured language;--"In which two voyage (of 1642 and 1644), he has given us reasonable contentment in respect to his services and the duties he has accomplished. It is therefore on account of this, at his request, and in consideration of his ability, also by reason of his having been again about six years in the country; and, moreover, that we find in him the spirit to render further good service to the General Council on like occasions in searching for rich countries for profitable trade".

IV.--TASMAN'S LATER YEARS, 1644-1659.

Tasman's failure to find what the Governor-General and the East India Company wanted--immediate and profitable trade--seems to have brought him under a cloud. He remained at Batavia, but without any important employment. In October, 1644, he and Frans Visscher laid down a route for an expedition fitted out to attack the Spanish ships coming from America to Manilla. But Visscher only was employed on the expedition, and Martin de Vries in a subsequent one. Tasman was passed over..

Governor-General Van Diemen died in 1645, and with him the era of great discovery expeditions closed. His successors in the government were not animated by the same zeal for exploration and adventure, but devoted their attention to strictly commercial matters, and Tasman found small opportunity for distinguishing himself. He was not wholly neglected. He was appointed (2nd November, 1644) a member of the Council of Justice at Batavia. It seems a somewhat inappropriate post for a sailor, but the special functions allotted to him may explain the appointment, for the resolution proceeds, "Commissioning and qualifying the said Tasman to demand and search for the journals of all incoming ships, and to report to us therefrom what is proper." He still held this post in December, 1646, but this did not prevent his occasional employment on more important and doubtless more congenial expeditions. Thus, in September, 1646, we find him sailing as Captain Commander in a mission to Djambi in Sumatra, and in August, 1647, going to Siam charged with letters from the Company to the King. He still kept up his relations with the Home Country, as there is mention on more than one occasion of his remitting sums of money to Holland. That he was a man of good repute amongst his fellow citizens is evidenced by the fact that in January, 1648, he was elected an Elder of the Reformed Congregation at Batavia.[*1]

After four years of comparative inactivity, he was once more entrusted with an important expedition. On 14th May, 1648, he took command of a fleet of eight ships, with 1150 men, which was to proceed to Manilla to lie in wait for the Spanish silver ships from America, to do what mischief it could to the enemy, and afterwards to sail to Siam. A further object was the suppression of the Chinese trade to Manilla and the extension of the Company's monopoly. The expedition was expected to accomplish great things for the Company. The Governor-General gave a dinner party to the officers on the eve of their departure and the fleet left Batavia confident of success. The result did not justify their hopes. A descent was made on the island of Luzon (or Manilla), a number of villaes and monasteries were pillaged and destroyed, and a rich village carried off, but the main object of the enterprise was not accomplished. The Chinese trade was not suppressed, neither did the Dutch fleet capture the silver ships. One of the Dutch vessels was wrecked in a storm, and the Spanish ships contrived to escape. Tasman reached Siam in November, and the conclusion of the Peace of Westphalia, which brought to an end the Eighty Years War between Spain and the United Netherlands, put a stop to further hostilities.

[*1] The Church Consistory at Batavia was a body which exercised a great influence in the Dutch East Indies. During the time Tasman sat as a member, a subject much discussed by the Consistory was a proposal for the suppression of Chinese idolatry, the destruction of all Chinese temples, and the punishment of the Priests. In April, 1648, the Consistory sent a Missionary, Dr. Hambroek, to Formosa, where he was shortly afterwards killed by the natives.--(Lauts, p. 290.)]

The fleet returned to Batavia in. January, 1649. An incident had occurred during the expedition which led to Tasman being tried before the Criminal Court, 23rd November, 1649. It is interesting, as giving us one of the few personal glimpses we have of the man, and as showing the severity with which the Company visited the delinquencies of their most valued officers, and vindicated the right of their meanest servants to a fair trial even in war time. It must be confessed that the incident does not present our navigator in a favourable light. According to the statement of the Advocate Fiscal, or prosecuting counsel, the facts were as follow:--In August, 1648, Tasman had landed at the Baviauw Islands with a military force, and had pitched a camp. He had issued orders that no one was to go outside the limits of the camp under pain of capital punishment. On the next day, "after he and some of his officers had all day been making good cheer at a certain monastery," on their return in the evening they came upon one of the supernumeraries and another sailor rambling outside the camp. Tasman was furious. He ordered the delinquents to be seized, and sentenced them to be hanged on the spot. He himself prepared the rope, and put it round the neck of the supernumerary, and made his Vice-Commander, Ogel, climb a tree and make fast the rope. This done, Tasman himself drew away the bench on which the man was standing, and left him hanging from the tree. He then made a rope ready for the second man. Luckily Ogel let go "the patient," but only just in time. Tasman made some defence, but the Court set it aside, and decided that not even the exigencies of war could excuse the Commander for hanging a man without a trial. The punishment inflicted was exemplary. Tasman was sentenced to be suspended from his office of Commander during the Governor-General's pleasure, to pay a. compensation of 1000 reals to the relatives of the sailor, a tine of 150 reals, and the costs of suit. In addition to this, he was to stand bareheaded in open Court, and publicly declare that lie had unjustly and unlawfully, without form of trial, of his own mere pleasure, and with his own hands, infamously executed the aforesaid innocent Coenraad Janssen of Amsterdam. It would appear that he was at the same time removed from his office in the Church Consistory--at least his name does not appear in the list of elders for the ensuing year.

The suspension from office lasted two years. In October, 1650, we find him again employed as Commander, and on the 5th January, 1651, by a resolution of the Governor-General and Council of India, he was formally reinstated in his rank, his reappointment to date from the 24th September preceding, when it is said he had again began to serve the Company.

After this time we have little information about him. It would appear that he considered his services were not sufficiently recognised, or at least that lie had grievances which he laid before the Council of Seventeen in Holland. In October, 1651, the Directors ordered that a letter of complaint from Abel Jansz Tasman be enquired into and reported on, but the result of the enquiry does not appear. In January, 1653, be wrote again to the Directory, the Colonial authorities curtly noting in the margin, "Abel Jansz Tasman fails to prove his rash assertions." Whatever his grievance was, it is evident that he failed to obtain satisfaction, and that it led to his retirement from the Company's service. The daily journal of Fort Batavia two months later records, under date 15th March, 1653, the arrival at Djapara of "Ex-Commander Tasman" in his own private vessel.

Of his last days we know nothing, except that he was a substantial and well-to-do citizen of Batavia, living just outside the town on the

Tygersgracht (Tiger Canal), one of the best and wealthiest quarters, and that lie had considerable landed property. There were only a few larger landholders in the town, amongst them Francois Caron, Chief Councillor for India and Director-General, who has been mentioned as head of the Dutch Factory in Japan in 1640. Lauts found from a contemporary map of Batavia that Tasman owned a pleasure garden of nearly six acres in one quarter, and no less than 282 acres on the Tiger's Canal, where he resided. Nieuwhoff; who was in the Indies from 1654 to 1670, says that the handsomest buildings in Batavia were situated on the Tiger's Canal, which was planted on both sides with fine trees. Valentyn says: "The view of this straight canal, so beautifully planted, surpasses anything I have ever seen in Holland."

On 10th April, 1657, Tasman made his will, which is still preserved in the Registry of the Probate Court of Batavia. It opens with the quaint old formula, "In the name of God, Amen!" and states that the testator is up and about, sick in body, but having good memory and understanding, and being used to think upon the shortness of life, that there is nothing more certain than death, and nothing more uncertain than the hour of the same, he has therefore resolved to make a solemn testament. First he beqeaths twenty-five guilders to the poor of Luytgegarst, his native village; secondly to Abel Heylman, his daughter's son, living in Batavia, a gold cup and silver-mounted sword. All the remainder of his property he gives to his beloved wife, Joanna Tjercx. If however she marries again, half of her bequest is to go over to the children of his only daughter, Claesjen. If his daughter or her children dispute the will, or require accounts from the widow, then their half share is to be reduced to one-fourth (the ordinary legal portion of a child). After his widow's death the half is to fall to the children of Claesjen; but as to the widow's half she may use and treat it as her own free property without contradiction of any.

Tasman had no children by his second wife, Joanna Tjercx. Claesjen was the daughter of his first wife, Claesgie Heyndricks. Claesjen had been twice married and had children by both husbands. The first, Philip Heylman, held an important office in the Fort; the second, Jacob Breemer, was an officer of the Probate Court of Batavia.

In October, 1659, the will was deposited in the Probate Court of Batavia; so that Tasman must have died in that year, fifteen years after his second great voyage.

The great navigators have seldom been long lived. Magellan and Cook died at fifty-one, Vasco da Gama at fifty-six. Tasman reached the latter age.

His widow, though forty-seven years old at her husband's death, did not long remain unconsoled. Eighteen months later, under date 5th February, 1661, the daily journal of Batavia records that permission was granted for the marriage of Jan Meynderts Springer, burgher of Batavia, to Madame Anna Tjerks, widow of the deceased Commander Abel Tasman, to be celebrated at her sick bed in consideration of her severe illness; Springer to pay to the Church a hundred reals of eight for the privilege.

It remains to mention the well-known story of Tasman's supposed attachment to a daughter of Governor-General Van Diemen, evidenced by his naming various places, e.g. Cape Maria Van Diemen, Maria Island, Maria Bay at Tonga. Flinders first suggested this little romance in his Voyage to Terra Australis, published in 1814. It pleased the fancy of the French geographer Eyries somewhere about 1820, and has been repeated and enlarged upon for some eighty years.

It is a pretty story, but unfortunately for the romance it has not the slightest foundation. In the light of recent investigations Tasman appears as a twice-married man of middle age, with a grown-up daughter. But this is not conclusive. Perhaps the next argument against the story is more cogent: Van Diemen had no daughter. If, however, anyone, is still unconvinced, we may clinch the argument with the express statement of Tasman attached to one of the drawings in his Journal:--"We have named this bay Maria Bay in compliment to the wife of Governor-General Van Diemen." If anyone after this requires further proof, let him consult the papers of the Dutch East India Company, or continue to write sentiment on the ardent young sailor's unrequited love.

To conclude. Tasman's discoveries, great as they were from a geographical point of view, bore no fruit for more than a hundred years. His tracks were marked on the chartg, but as to the countries he discovered, his countrymen in the East Indies, whose sole object was trade, felt no temptation to explore the wild bush of Van Diemen's Land, or to face the fierce tribes of Massacre Bay, or even to plant colonies on the barren and inhospitable shores of Western Australia peopled by naked savages. Only the Englishman Dampier in 1688, and again in 1699, visited the western coast, and was glad to leave what he described as the most miserable country on earth. Had Tasman but discovered the way through Torres Strait, it is possible that New South Wales might have been colonised by the Dutch. It was reserved, however, for an English navigator, more than a century after Tasman's voyage, to make the practical discovery of Australia as a land for European colonisation. When Captain Cook in his first famous voyage in the Endeavour, on Sunday, 29th April, 1770, cast anchor in Botany Bay, the Australian Continent was first laid open to European enterprise; eighteen years later Sydney was founded by Englishmen. Would that the first planting of these Colonies had been other than it was, and that the wise warning of Lord Bacon had been heeded; for, says he--"It is a shameful and unblessed thing to take the scum of the people and wicked condemned men to be the people with whom you plant; and not only so, but it spoileth the plantation, for they will ever live like rogues and not fall to work, but be lazy, and do mischief, and spend victuals and be quickly weary, arid then certify over to their country to the discredit of the plantation." All which things were verified in the early history of these Colonies. But Australia "has burst her birth's invidious bar, and grasped the skirts of happy chance; breasted the blows of circumstance, and grappled with her evil star; has made by force her merit known, and lived to clutch the golden keys." A hundred years growth has now made Australia well nigh a nation; but as yet it is a nation in the gristle only. When the petty jealousies of the Colonies are laid aside, and when the several States.--as we hope may soon be the case--are united in one great Federation, we may feel a perfect confidence that, amongst the children of the old English mother, not the least important will be those dwelling in the island Continent circumnavigated by Tasman two hundred and fifty years ago, who will claim the title of Citizens of the Commonwealth of Australia.

BIBLIOGRAPHICAL NOTES, MAPS OF THE VOYAGES, 1642 AND 1644.

Manuscript Maps.

1. In the collection of Van Keulen of Amsterdam. A large and handsome map on Japanese paper, showing both voyages. Mr. Leupe thinks it to be the work of Pilot-Major Visscher. Australia bears the name of Compagnis Nieu Nederlandt. This map was reproduced in coloured facsimile in Mr. Swart's edition of the complete journal published in 1860.

2. In the British Museum. Sloane MSS. 5222, Art. 12. A large sketch map, roughly executed, showing both voyages. In the centre of Australia is written "This large Land of New Guinea was first discovered to joyne to ye South Land by ye Yot Lemmen as by this Chart Ffrançois Jacobus Vis. Pilot Maior Anno 1643." Mr. Major, who gives a reduced copy of this chart in his Early Voyages, thinks it to be a copy of a map by Visscher, and that it was made by Captain Thomas Bowrey, of Fort St. George, about 1687. Mr. Alfred Mault, of Hobart, has made a facsimile of the original map, and this has been photo-lithographed for the Royal Society of Tasmania.

3. In the India Museum, South Kensington. A coloured chart of the coast of Van Diemen's Land, endorsed in an old hand: "A Draught of the South Land lately discovered, 1643." Mr. A. Mault found this chart amongst the Records of the India Office. He contributed to the Transactions of the Australasian Association for the Advancement of Science, 1892, a description of this map with coloured facsimile.

Early Maps.

In 1648, four years after Tasman's second voyage, the building of the new Stadhuis, or Town Hall, of Amsterdam was begun. The opportunity was taken to commemorate Tasman's discoveries by showing them in a great map of the world in two hemispheres, cut in the stone pavement of the Great Hall (Burgerzaal) of the Stadhuis. This pavement has long since been boarded over.

Mr. Major says that an outline of the coast visited by Tasman is given in Turquet's Mappemonde, published in Paris in 1647; also in the 1650 edition of Janssen's Atlas, and in the 1660 edition of J. Klencke's Atlas. The discoveries are also shown in Fredk. de Wit's map, published in 1660; and a representation of the hemispheres is given in the fine work describing the Stadhuis, and published in 1661. The map in Thévenot (1663) is from the Stadhuis pavement, but with names added. Some of the published maps contain the names Hollandia Nova and Zeelandia Nova.

MANUSCRIPTS OF THE JOURNAL OF 1642.

Mr. Leupe describes three. contemporary manuscripts which are preserved in Holland:--

1. R.A. 1. In the State Archives at the Hague. Consists of 28 double folio leaves, bound in a volume which forms part of a collection made by Cornelis Sweers. It is badly written and kept in a slovenly manner, probably by a young officer on board the Heemskerrk.

2. R.A. 2. In the State Archives. In a large folio volume containing 196 pages, very neatly written, with a large number of charts and drawings, some coloured. It bears the autograph signature of Tasman, and is apparently a fair copy of the official journal kept on board the Heemskerck. It is probably the manuscript used by Valentyn in compiling his account. He reproduced most of the maps and sketches. This manuscript, with the charts and drawings, is to be reproduced in facsimile in Messrs. Fred. Muller & Co's. forthcoming edition.

3. H. v. M. In the possession of Mr. Huydecoper van Marsseveen. In a folio volume, smaller than R.A. 2, contains 112 pages, neatly written, with three small charts and some sketches. It also is a copy of an original journal, and is not signed. It has some particulars not given in R.A. 2. It is from Cornelis Sweers' collection.

The following manuscripts are also known:--

4. Brit. M us. 8946. Plut. C.L. xxii. D. In the British Museum. It is carelessly written, and contains 38 charts and sketches. Probably a copy of R.A. 2. This manuscript was bought in London at Mr. Lloyd's sale, some time before 1776, for half-ag-uinea, and was subsequently acquired by Sir Joseph Banks. In 1776 Banks employed the Revd. Charles G. Woide, Chaplain of the Dutch Chapel at St. James's, to translate it. Woide's translation was used by Captain Burney in his

work. About 1868 the late Mr. J. E. Calder published in the Tasmanian Times the account of the discovery of Tasmania taken from Burney.

5. Amongst the hydrographical documents belonging to the publishing firm of Van Keulen of Amsterdam, there was formerly a manuscript copy of the Journal. It was probably a copy agreeing with R.A. 2, and, it is said, bore Tasman's signature. Mr. Swart printed the complete Journal from this copy, 1854-59.

6. Mr. Lauts mentions that a manuscript copy of the Journal was bought by the bookseller Born, of Amsterdam, in 1835.

PRINTED WORKS.

Principal Collections of Voyages containing an abstract of the Journal of 1642.

1. Nierop, Dirck Rembrantsz van-Een kort verhael uyt het journaal van der kommander Abel Jansen Tasman in 't ontdekken van 't onbekende Suit Landt in 't jare 1642. (A short account from the journal of Commander A. J. Tasman on the discovery of the unknown South Land in the year 1642). 4to. Amsterdam, 1669-74.**[*1]**

[The first published abstract of the Journal. Nos. 2 to 9, are translations of this.]

2. Hooke, Dr. Robert-Philosophical Collections. 4to. London, 1678.**[*1]**

3. Thévenot, Melchisedek-Relation de divers voyages curieux. Nouvelle edition. 2 vols., fol.: Paris, 1696.
[The first edition 1663-72 contains the map only. The voyage was printed as a supplement, circa 1681.]

4. An Account of several late Voyages and Discoveries. 8vo: London, 1694. 2nd edition, 1711. [Narbrough's Voyage, &c.]

5. Harris, Dr. John-Collection of Voyages and Travels. Fol.: London, 1702-05.

6. Campbell, Dr. John-Navigantium atque itinerantium bibliotheca, by John Harris. 2 vols, fol.: London, 1744-48. [With notes and map].

7. Voyages de F. Coreal aux Indes Occidentales. 3 vols., 12mo: Amsterdam, 1722: Paris, 1738. [The voyage is appended as a supplement].

8. Brosses, Charles de-Histoire des Navigations aux Terres Australes. 2 vols., 4to: Paris, 1756. [With Vaugondy's map of Australasia].

9. Callander, John-Terra Australis Cognita. 3 vols., 8vo: Edinburgh, 1766-68.

10. Valentyn, François-Oud en Nieuw Oost-Indien (Old and New East Indies), 5 vols., fol.: Dordrecht, 1724-26. [A much fuller account taken from the original journal, with reproductions of many drawings and maps].

11. Prévost, L'Abbé Antoine François-Histoire generale des Voyages. 19 vols., 4to: Paris, 1746-70.**[*1]**

12. Du Bois, J. P. J.-Histoire générale des Voyages. 25 vols., 4to: The Hague, 1747-80. [De Hondt's Collection].

13. De Hondt, Pieter-Historische beschryving der reizen. 21 vols., 4to: The Hague, 1747-67.

14. Dalrymple, Alexander-Historical Collection of the several Voyages and Discoveries in the South Pacific Ocean. 2 vols., 4to: London, 1770-71. [The text is taken from Valentyn, collated with Nos. 2, 3, 4, 6, and 12].

[*1) Works which the present writer has not seen are distinguished by an asterisk at end of title.]

15. Burney, Captain James--Chronological History of the Discoveries in the South Sea. 5 vols., 4to: London, 1803-17. [The narrative is taken from Sir Joseph Banks' manuscript mentioned above].

16. Eyries, J. B., and Malte Brun--Nouvelles Annales des Voyages. 44 vols., 8vo: Paris, 1819-28.**[*1]**

Books and Articles relating to Tasman.

Witsen, Nicolas--Noord en Oost Tartarye (North and East Tartary). 2 vols., Amsterdam, 1705.**[*1]**

[Contains some particulars of voyage of 1644].

Du Bois, J. P. J.--Vie des Gouverneurs Généraux, avec l'abrégé de l'histoire des établissemens Hollandois aux Indes Occidentales. 4to: The Hague, 1763.
[Contains life and portrait of Van Diemen].

Flinders, Captain Matthew--Voyage to Terra Australis, 1801-3. 2 vols., 4to and atl. fol. London, 1814.

Moll, Ger.--Verhandeling over eenige vroegere Zeetogten der Nederlanders. (Essay on some earlier voyages of the Dutch.) 8vo: Amsterdam, 1825.

Siebold, Ph. Fras. von--Documens importans sur la découverte des îles de Bonin par les navigateurs Néerlandais [Quast et Tasman] en 1639. 8vo pamph.: The Hague, 1843.[*1]

Swart, Jacob--Cook en Columbus...met bijvoeging van den Nederlandschen ontdekker A. J. Tasman--(Cook and Columbus, with an addition respecting the Dutch discoverer A. J. Tasman.) In Tindal and Swart's Verhandelingen, &c. (Papers on Nautical Affairs). N.S., Vol. 3. 8vo: Amsterdam, 1843.

Swart, Jacob--Instructie of Lastbrief voor den Schipper Commandeur A. J. Tasman in 1644. (Instructions or Commission for the Captain Commander, &c.) In Tindal and Swart's Verhandelingen, &c. N.S., Vol. 4. 8vo: Amsterdam, 1844.

Lauts, 0.--Abel Jansz. Tasman. In Tindal and Swart's Verhandelingen, &c. N.S., Vol. 4. 8vo: Amsterdam, 1844.

Gell, Rev. John Philip--On the first Discovery of Tasmania in November and December, 1642, In Tasmanian Journal of Natural Science, Vol. 2: London, 1845.

Boekeren, G. R. Voormeulen van--Reizen en ontdekkingstogten van A. J. Tasman, van Lutkegast. (Voyages and discovery expeditions of, &c.) 16mo: Groningen, 1849.

Calder, James Erskine--Some account of that part of Forestier's Peninsula, Tasmania, visited by A. J. Tasman in 1642. The Hobart Town Courier, 24th November, 1849.

Siebold, Ph. Fras. von--Geschichte der Entdeckungen im Seegebiete von Japan. (History of the discoveries in the Japan Seas.) 4to and atlas: Leyden, 1851-52.

Leupe, P. A.--Abel J. Tasman en Franchoys Jacobsz Visscher: 1642-1644. In- Bijdragen tot de taal- land- en volkenkunde van Nederlandsch-Indië. (Contributions to the philology, geography, and ethnography of Netherlands-India.) Vol, 4. Amsterdam, 1856.

[*1) Works which the present writer has not seen are distinguished by an asterisk at end of title.]

Major, Richard H.--Early Voyages to Terra Australis, now called Australia. 8vo: London (Hakluyt Society), 1859.

Swart, Jacob--Journaal van de reis naar het Onbekende Zuidland in den jaar 1642, door A. J. Tasman. (Journal of the voyage to the Unknown South Land in the year 1642, by A. J. Tasman.) 8vo: Amsterdam, 1860.

Chijs, J. van der, and Norman, H. D. L.--In Tijdschrift voor dische taal- &c. kunde. (Journal of Indian philology, &c.), Vol. 12. 8vo: Amsterdam, 1862.[*1]

Leupe, P. A.--De Reizen der Nederlanders naar het Zuidland of Nieuw Holland in de 17e en 18e eeuwen. (The voyages of the Dutch to the South Land or New Holland in the 17th and 18th centuries.) 8vo: Amsterdam, 1868.

Leupe, P. A.--De Handschriften der ontdekkingreis van A. J. Tasman en F. J. Visscher: 1642-1643. (The manuscripts of the discovery voyage of A. J. Tasman and F. J. Visscher.) In Fruin's Bijdragen voor vaderlandsche geschiedenis, &c.) (Contributions for the history, &c. of the Fatherland). V01. 7. 8vo: Amsterdam, 1872.

Dozy, Chas. M.--Abel Janszoon Tasman. In Bijdragen tot de taal- &c. kunde, &c., 5th series, Vol. 2. 8vo: The Hague, 1887.

Walker, James B.--The Discovery of Tasmania in 1642; with Notes on the localities mentioned in Tasman's Journal of the Voyage. In Papers, &c. of The Royal Society of Tasmania for 1890. 8vo: Hobart, 1891.

Mault, Alfred.--On an old Manuscript Chart of Tasmania in the Records of the India Office. In Transactions of the Australian Association for the Advancement of Science for 1892. 8vo: Hobart, 1892.

Heeres, J. E.--Abel Janszoon Tasman. In Groningsche Volksalmanak voor het jaar 1893. (Groningen People's Almanac for the year 1893). 8vo: Groningen, 1893.

Stamperius, J.--Abel Tasman. 8vo Haarlem, 1893.[*1]

Hocken Dr. T. M.--Abel Tasman and his Journal. Paper read before the Otago Institute, 10th September, 1895. 8vo, pamph.: Dunedin, 1895.

Heeres, J. E., and Coote, C. H. Abel Jansz Tasman's Journal of his discovery of Van Diemen's Land and New Zealand in 1642, with documents relating to his exploration of Australia in 1644; being photo-lithographic facsimiles of the original manuscripts at The Hague and elsewhere, with English translation. Edited, with introduction, biographical and geographical notes, by J. E. Heeres, of the Dutch State Archives, and C. H. Coote, of the British Museum. 53 maps and designs. Folio: Amsterdam, Frederik Muller & Co. (In the press.)**[*1]**

[*1) Works which the present writer has not seen are distinguished by an asterisk at end of title.]

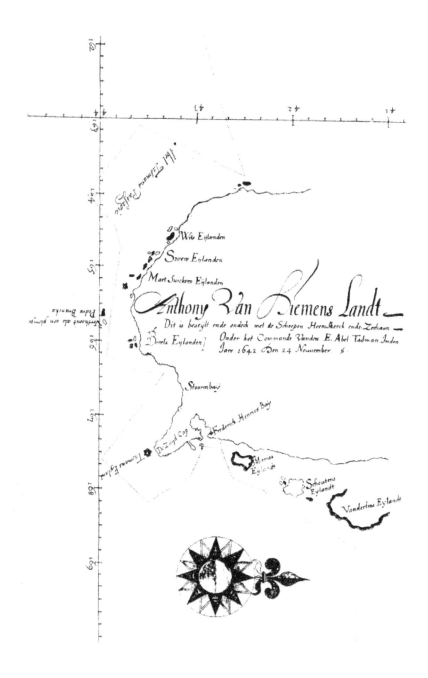

Anthony Van Diemens Landt

Dit is besegelt ende ondeck met de Scheepen Heemskerck ende Zeehaen
Onder het Commande Vanden E. Abel Tasman Inden
Jarr 1642 Den 24 November 8

Wits Eylanden
Sovern Eylanden
Mart Suyckers Eylanden

Boerels Eylanden

Stoormbaij

Frederick Hennes Baij

De Zuyd Cap

Maria Eylandt

Schoutens Eylandt

Vanderlins Eylandt

APPENDIX. THE DISCOVERY OF TASMANIA.

FROM TASMAN'S JOURNAL, 1642.[*1]

23rd November.[*2]--Good weather, and the wind S.W., with a fresh gale. In the morning found that our rudder-head was broken in two in the tiller-mortise; whereupon lay to under shortened sail, and put a plank on either side. Noon, found our latitude 42° 50', and longitude 162° 51'. Course held E., and sailed 25 (100) miles. Here found one degree north-westerly variation, which here decreases very rapidly. According to our reckoning had the west side of Nova Guinea to the north of us.

24th November.--Good weather and clear sky. Noon, found latitude 42° 25', and longitude 163° 31'. Course kept E. by N., and sailed 30 (120) miles. The wind from the S.W., and afterwards S., with a gentle top-gallant breeze. Afternoon, about 4 o'clock, saw land. Had it E. by N. from us 10 (40) miles by our reckoning. It was very high land. Towards evening saw in the E.S.E. three high mountains, and in the N.E. also saw two mountains, but not so high as those to the south. Here had a true pointing compass. In the evening, in the first glass when the watch[*3] was set (8 P.M.), proposed to the council of our ship with the under mates, whether it would not be best to stand off the shore to sea; and required their opinion, when they thought this to be most advisable. Whereupon unanimously approved after 3 glasses (9.30 P.M.) to lie out from the shore and run from it 10 glasses (5 hours), when we should stand back to the land: all more fully appearing in the resolution of this date to which we refer. At night, after 3 glasses (1½ hours), the wind was S.E. Tacked from the shore, and sounded in 100 fathoms, clean white fine sand with small shells; afterwards sounded again, and had black coarse sand with small stones. At night had the wind S.E. with gentle breeze.

25th November.--Morning, nearly calm. Hoisted the white flag and the flag at the mizzen-top-gallant-mast, whereupon the officers of the *Zeehaen*--with their mates came on board us, when we called the council and resolved with them, as is to be seen by the resolution of this day, and is there set out at length, to which we here refer. Towards noon got the wind S.E., and afterwards S.S.E. and S. Tacked for the shore. In the evening, about 5 o'clock, came under the shore. Three miles (12) out from the shore had 60 fathoms, coral bottom

[*1] Translated from SWART'S edition of the Journal, with notes, &c., published at Amsterdam in 1860. A strictly literal translation has been preferred, as giving a better idea of the quaintness of the original.]

[*2] The days are reckoned from midnight to midnight. The longitude is calculated from the meridian of the *Peak of Teneriffe*.]

[*3] The first watch MS from 8 P.M. to midnight. A half-hour sand-glass was used to measure the time.]

1 mile out (4 miles) had clean fine white sand. Found this coast stretching S. by E. and N. by W., a smooth [bare] coast, and had reached latitude 42° 30', and mean longitude 163° 50'. Tacked again from the shore. The wind blew S.S.E., topgallant breeze. When you come from the W. and find that you have 4° north-westerly variation, then you may look out for land, because the variation here decreases very rapidly. If it happens that you get rough weather from the westerly quarter, then you may well lie to, and not sail ahead. Here on the coast you have a compass pointing true. We have also the mean longitude, which we determined by each working out his reckoning and taking the mean. Wherefrom we find this land to be in the longitude of 163° 50'.

This land is the first land in the *South Sea* (*Zuytzee*) that we have met with, and is yet known by no European nations. So we have given this land the name of ANTHOONY VAN DIEMENSLANDT, in honor of the Most Honorable the Governor-General, our High Master, who sent us out to make these discoveries. The islands lying round about it, as many as are known to us, we have named after the Honorable Members of the Council of India, and may be seen on the small chart made thereof.

[Here there are in the manuscript some sketches of land, of which two are found in VALENTYN, p. 48, No. 1A and No. 5E. The other, No. 5E; I have not found in the manuscript.--JACOB SWART.]

26th November.--Had the wind easterly, gentle breeze, hazy weather, so that we could not see land. Reckoned we were about 9 (38) miles from the shore. Towards noon, hoisted the flag at the main-top-gallant-Mast, whereupon the Zeehaen immediately came up under our stern, when we hailed her people that Sr. GILSEMANS should come aboard. Whereupon the said GILSEMANS without delay came on board us, and we made known to him the matters which are mentioned in the under-written note, and are to be taken with him to his ship, in order to show the same to the Skipper, GERRIT JANSZ, and also for orders to their mates.

"The officers of the fly-ship Zeehaen shall in their daily log describe this land, which we saw yesterday and are now near, as in longitude 163° 50'--because by mutual reckoning we find it thus, and this longitude as settled--and begin to reckon the longitude afresh from thence. He who before this has longitude 160° or more, shall now make his reckoning from that land. This is therefore done in order to avoid all mistakes as much as is in any way possible. The officers of the Zeehaen shall give the same charge to the mates, and shall also observe it, because we find this to be fitting; and the charts which are hereafter made by any one shall lay down that land in the mean longitude as before stated of 163° 50'.

"Given on the *Heemshercq*, date as above.

"(Undersigned) ABEL JANSZ TASMAN."

Noon, reckoned we were in S. latitude 43° 36', and longitude 163° 2'. Course kept S.S.W., and sailed 18 (72) miles. Had half a degree north-westerly variation. Got the wind N.E. Set our course E.S.E.

27th November.--Morning, saw the coast again. Our course was still E.S.E. Noon, reckoned we were in S. latitude 44° 4', and longitude 164° 2'. Course held S.E. by E., and sailed 13 (52) miles. It was drizzling, misty, hazy, and rainy weather the wind N.E. and N.N.E., with gentle breeze. At night, after 7 glasses in the first watch (11.30 P.M.), lay to under shortened sail. We dared not sail on, by reason that it was so dark.

28th November.--Morning, still cloudy, misty, rainy weather. Made sail again. Set our course E., and afterwards N.E. by N. Saw land N.E. and N.N.E. from us, and stood straight for it. The coast here stretches S.E. by E. and N.W. by W. This land runs away here to the east so far as I can observe. Noon, by reckoning in latitude 44° 12', and longitude 165° 2'; and course held E. by S., and sailed 11 (44) miles. The wind from the N.W., with gentle breeze. In the evening came under the shore. There are under the shore some small islands, one of which looks like a lion. This lies about 3 (12) miles out to sea from the mainland. Evening got the wind E. At night lay to under shortened sail.

29th November.--Morning, were still near the rock which looks like a lion's head.[*1] Had the wind westerly, with topgallant breeze. Sailed along the coast, which here stretches east and west. Towards noon passed two rocks, the most westerly looking like *Pedra Branca*, which lies on the coast of *China*; the most easterly, looking like a high rugged tower, lies about 4 (16) miles out from the mainland. Ran through between these rocks and the land. Noon, reckoned we were in latitude 43° 53', longitude 166° 3'. Course held E.N.E., and sailed 12 (48) miles. Still sailed along the shore. In the evening, about 5 o'clock, came before a bay.[*1] It seemed that we would likely find a good anchorage there. Wherefore resolved with our ships' council to run into it, as appears by the said resolution. Were almost in the bay when there presently arose such a violent wind that we were obliged to take in our sails and run back to sea under shortened sail, because it was impossible with such a wind to come to an anchor. In the evening resolved to stand out to sea for the night under shortened sail that we might not fall on a lee shore in such a storm. All which is to be seen more at large in the above-mentioned resolution, whereto (to avoid prolixity) we here refer.

[*1) The *Mewstone*.]

Ultimo November.--Morning, at dawn, tacked to the shore. Had been driven off from the shore so far by wind and current that we could scarcely see land. Did our best to approach it again. Noon, had land N.W. from us; tacked to the west, the wind northerly, but not serving us to fetch the land. Noon, found latitude 43° 41', longitude 168° 3'. Course held E. by N., and sailed 20 (80) miles, with stormy and unsettled weather. Here the compass showed true. A little after noon tacked to the west, with hard unsteady breeze. Tacked to the north under shortened sail.

Primo December.--Morning, weather somewhat more moderate. Set our topsails; the wind W.S.W., with top-gallant breeze. Steered our course for the shore. Noon, found latitude 43° 10', and longitude 167° 55'. Course held N.N.W., and sailed 8 (32) miles, and was almost calm. At noon, hoisted the white flag, whereupon our friends of the *Zeehaen* came on board, when we resolved together that it would be best and most expedient, if wind and weather but permitted, to get on land, the sooner the better, so as to obtain a nearer knowledge of its situation, and also to see what refreshments were to be had, as the resolution of to day shows more at large. Afterwards got a little breeze from the eastward. Ran towards the shore to examine whether some good anchorage can be got hereabouts. About an hour after sunset let go the anchor in a good harbour, in 22 fathoms, between white and grey fine sand, good holding ground; for which we must show thankful hearts to Almighty God.

[Here in TASMAN'S Journal is the little map found in VALE NTYN, pp. 48, 49. The degrees of longitude in VALENTYN differ one whole degree from those in TASMAN'S Journal. Also the two little ships of the latter are not found in the little map in the Journal.--JACOB SWART.]

[*1) *Storm bay*, or rather, *Adventure Bay*.]

2nd December.--Early in the morning sent the Pilot-Major, FRANCOY JACOBSZ, with our long-boat (*chaloup*), with 4 musketeers and 6 rowers, every one provided with a pike and sidearms, together with the launch (*praeutien, sloep*) of the Zeehaen, and one of their second mates and 6 musketeers, to an inlet (*innijck*), which was situated fully a long mile (Le., over 4 miles) north-west of us, in order to see what useful things--such as fresh water, refreshments, timber, and other things--might be obtainable there. About 3 hours before evening our boats returned, bringing various samples of vegetables, which they had seen growing in abundance, some not unlike certain herbs which grow at the *Cabo de Bona Esperance* (*Cape of Good Hope*) and are fit for use as pot herbs. Others were long and saltish, which have no ill-likeness to sea-parsley. The Pilot-Major and the second-mate of the *Zeehaen* reported what follows, namely:--

That they had rowed above a mile (4 miles) to the said point, where they had found high but level land with herbs (not planted, but springing from God and nature), fruitful timber in plenty, and a running watering place, and many open valleys; which water was good indeed, but very troublesome to draw, and running so slowly that it could only be taken out with a bowl.

That they had heard some sound of people; also a playing nearly like a trumpet or small gom [gong], winch was not far from them, but they had not got to bee anyone.

That they had seen two trees about 2 to 2½ fathoms thick, 60 to 65 feet high below the branches, which trees had been hacked into with flints, and the bark peeled off in the form of steps (in order to climb up thereby and take birds' nests), each being full 5 feet from the other. So that they presumed that there were very tall men here, or that they must know how to climb the said trees by some device, In one tree these cut steps seemed so fresh and green as if not four days had passed since they had been hewn.

That they had observed in the earth footprints or scratchings of some beasts, not ill-resembling the claws of a tiger. They also brought on board some dung of four-footed beasts (as they presumed and could observe), besides a little gum, fine in appearance, which drops out of the trees, and has a resemblance to gumlac (*gomma lacca*). That about the east point of this bay, having sounded at high-water, they had found 13 to 14 feet; the ebb and flood there about 3 feet.

That in the entrance of the said point they had seen a multitude of gulls, wild ducks, and geese, but none landward: though they had indeed heard the noise of them; and had observed no fish, but divers mussels sticking in sundry places on bushes.

That the country is generally occupied with trees, which stand so thinly scattered that you may pass through everywhere and see to a far distance; so that you could always get sight of people or wild beasts in the country, as it is unencumbered by thick wood or underwood; which should give great facility for the exploring of the country.

That in various places in the interior they had seen many trees which had been deeply burnt into above their roots. The earth was here and there beaten down and burnt as hard as stones by the lighting of fires on it.

A little before our bouts (which were coming on board) got within sight, we saw at times a thick smoke rising on the land, which lay about W. by N. from us. We therefore presumed that our people were doing it for a signal, because they were delayed so long in returning; for they had their orders to come back to us with speed, partly in order to inform us of their discoveries, or otherwise, if they saw there was nothing useful there, that they might go to examine other places, so that no time should be spent uselessly. Our people having come on board we asked them whether they had been thereabouts and had lighted fires, whereupon they replied that they had not, but that at divers times and places in the woods they also had seen smokes; so that without doubt there must be men in this place, and these of an uncommon stature.

To-day, had much variable wind from the eastward, but the most of the day a stiff steady gale from the S.E.

3rd December.--To-day we went with the Merchant GILSEMANS and our boats, as yesterday, with musketeers, the rowers being provided with pikes and side arms, to the S.E. side of this bay. Where we found water, the land so low that the fresh water was made brackish and salt through the breaking of the sea, and the ground was too rocky to sink wells. Therefore returned on board, summoned the council of our two ships, with whom we resolved and found to be good, as is shown by the resolution of this date, where it is to be seen at length and is set forth; whereto for brevity's sake we here refer. Afternoon, we went with the said boats, together with the Pilot-Major FRANCOYS JACOBSZ, the Skipper GERRIT JANSZ, ISACK GILSEMANS, Merchant of the *Zeehaen*, the Junior Merchant ABRAHAM COOMANS; and our Chief Carpenter PIETER JACOBSZ, to the S.E. corner of this bay, having with us a pole with the Company's mark cut therein, and the Prince's flag, in order to set the same up there, so that it may be evident to posterity that we have been here and taken the said land for a possession and property. Having rowed with our boats about half way, it began to blow hard and the sea to rise so-high that the launch of the *Zeehaen*, in which were the Pilot-Major and Sr. GILSEMANS, was obliged to return on board. We went on with our long-boat (*chaloup*), coming close under the shore into a little hay which lay W.S.W. from the ships. The surf broke at such a rate that the land could not be approached without danger of the boat being dashed in pieces. We ordered the said carpenter to swim ashore by himself with the pole and Prince's flag, and remained with the long-boat lying to the wind. We made him set up the said pole with the flag at the top in the earth before a decaying tree, the lowest one of a group of four noticeable high trees standing in the form of a crescent about the middle of this bay. This tree is burnt just above the foot, and is indeed the tallest of the other three,[*1] though it appears to be not so high, since it stands on the declivity of the cluster. It has at the top above its crown two high dry branches sticking out, so uniformly set about with dry twigs and branchlets that it looks like the great horns of a stag.

Moreover, on the undermost side there stands a very green and round well-crowned branch, the shoots of which, by their even proportion, made the said tree very elegant and like the top of a larding pin. After the head carpenter had accomplished the matter above rehearsed, in view of me, ABEL JANSZ TASMAN, the Skipper GERRIT JANSZ, and the Junior Merchant ABRAHAM COOMANS, we rowed the boat as near to the shore as we dared venture, and the said carpenter swam back again to the longboat through the surf; when, after accomplishing this matter, we rowed back, again on board, leaving the above-mentioned as a memorial to posterity and to the inhabitants of this country, who did not show themselves, although we suspected that some of them were not far from there, and kept watchful eyes on our proceedings.

We did not look for herbs, for on account of the roughness of the sea no one could reach the shore save by swimming, so that it was impossible to bring anything to the long-boat. All day the wind was mostly northerly. In the evening took observation of the sun, and found 3° N.E. variation. With sunset got a strong north wind, which rapidly increased to so violent a storm from the N.N.W. that we were constrained to strike both yards and to let go our bower anchor.

4th December.--With the dawning of day the storm abated. The weather moderate, and the wind being off shore W. by N. Hove in the bower anchor again. The said anchor being hove up and got above water, saw that both flukes were so far gone that we got home nothing but the bare shaft. Weighed the other anchor also, and got under sail, in order to sail to the north between the most northerly islands, and to seek a more convenient watering-place. We have lain at anchor here in S. lat. 43°, long. 167½°. Before noon the wind westerly. At noon found lat. 42° 40', long. 168°. Course held. N.E., and sailed 8 (32) miles. Afternoon, the wind N.W. The whole day very variable winds. In the evening again had W.N.W. with strong wind, W. by N., and W.N.W. Tacked about to the northward. In the evening saw a round mountain N.N.W. of us about 8 (32) miles. Course close hauled by the wind northwards. In sailing out of this bay, and also the whole day through, saw away along the coast much smoke rising from fires. We should here describe the trend of the coast and of the neighbouring islands, but excuse the same in order to be brief, referring to the small chart that has been made of it, and is subjoined herewith.

[*1) *Sic* in original.]

[Here is probably meant the chart of which mention is made in the conclusion of this Journal for 1st December.--JACOB SWART.]

5th December.--In the morning the wind N.W. by W. Still made our course as before. The high round mountain which we had seen the day 'before bore due W. of us 6 (24) miles, from whence the land falls off to the N.W. so that we could no longer hold could land on board, because the wind was almost ahead. Wherefore we summoned the Council and second mates, who proposed, and it was therewith resolved---the officers of the *Zeehaen* having been spoken--to set our course due east, according to the resolution of the 11th ulto., and to run on this course until we reach the longitude of 195°, or that of the *Salomonis Islands*, as may be more fully seen by the resolution of this date. Noon, reckoned lat. 41° 34', long. 169°. Course held N.E. by and sailed 20 (80) miles. Set our course due east, in order to make further discoveries, and also in order not to fall into the variable winds between the trades and counter-trades. The wind N.W., fresh gale. At night the wind W., strong fresh gale and good clear weather.

THE END

Made in the USA
Middletown, DE
09 August 2023